JESUS:
A MAN'S MAN

To Kaely,
I hope you enjoy my book!
Keep Jesus First
(Matthew 6:33)
Bria

B R I A N   V A N   C L E A V E

ISBN 978-1-68570-932-7 (paperback)
ISBN 978-1-68570-933-4 (digital)

Christian Faith Publishing
832 Park Avenue
Meadville, PA 16335
www.christianfaithpublishing.com

Printed in the United States of America

To Jesus. Robann, forty-three years of marriage, and it keeps getting better.

My kids Brianna, Brian Jr., and Angie and their spouses.

The best grandkids in the world—Keeley, Trent, Landry, Sawyer, Tanner, Addison, Kylie, and Payton.

FOREWORD

"I'm going to write a book." Oh, if I had a dollar for every time someone has told me that. Teaching middle-school English for more than thirty years means I've heard that phrase in so many forms I could write a book, but Brian meant it. I remember clearly we were standing in the sea of students, watching the ebb and flow of another passing period when he turned to me and in all seriousness outlined his idea. It seemed like a good plan; then he sprung "I need someone to look it over as I write. Would you do that?"

I remember chuckling at the idea of reading work not written by young teens as I answered with a "Sure thing." A few months later, he brought me a draft of chapter 1.

After reading, I was hooked. It appears that Mr. VC can tell a story—one that grabbed my attention and made me want to read the lessons that accompanied it. As I learned more about his family, his childhood friends, and his connection to biblical truths, I realized he not only had a few chapters written, but he had the makings of a complete book. A book that would be filled with personal struggle, triumph, and lessons learned both the hard way and the easy way. After finishing chapter 3, I had both laughed and learned; this was his purpose. Then Mr. VC retired. I thought fondly back on those few chapters. They'd been written for men, and while I grew up with boys and have spent more than three decades married to a man, I'm certainly not one. So when I realized one day that I was applying a lesson learned from his stories, I found myself not only finding new relevancy for his work but also wishing he had finished his writing.

Several years later, I got an email from Brian. He had more chapters; I was really excited. Apparently in the intervening years, he had been mulling ideas, and now they were pouring forth. Chapters

v

came to my inbox regularly; I printed them, wrote all over them, returned them, and learned. Over the years, my thinking has been challenged in my own Bible study classes, in conversations with my friend Lynn, and often in Sunday school as I teach freshman girls, but I'd never imagined that a book—even one filled with anecdotes, verses, and cleverly connected insights—would give me so much pause for thought. The prayer and guidance Brian illustrated in writing his book are reflected in the efficacy of his work.

By the time we got through the final chapter, I knew more about some of the men in the Bible, I knew more about some of the men in my life, and I knew more about my walk with my heavenly Father. Brian has given me (and each of us who read his work) personal stories with which we can connect and the godly lessons we can apply. I feel honored to have been asked to work with him and delighted that his work will have the opportunity to touch others.

Thanks, Mr. VC, for reminding all of us that our walk goes farther than we will ever know; may many be challenged, inspired, and blessed by your words.

Wendy Buhler
7/8 Language Arts/Literature
Dunway Middle School
Track and Field/Volleyball
McMinnville High School

ENDORSEMENTS

Brian Van Cleave's *Jesus, a Man's Man* captures the essence of the spiritual and human side of manhood from a scriptural and personal perspective. He brings together ten examples from Jesus's life on earth to explore how a man balances all the complexities involved in living the life of a strong and insightful man. The author shares fresh insight into the scriptural examples of what it is to grow as a man. He also brings his own experiences to demonstrate how he took these lessons from Jesus's life and applied them to his own for a deeper fulfillment of the balance of being a man. The lessons from *Jesus, a Man's Man* is for all who share the desire for spiritual balance in their lives, or in the life of a man whom the reader cares about.

—*Bruce Nichols LMSW*
Retired Captain of the Hutchinson Fire Department
Hutchinson, Kansas

Brian Van Cleave is a wonderful storyteller. He paints a clear, vivid picture as if you are really in the moment with him. As a Bible teacher, he brings the Word of God to life. It's relatable, real, and applicable. This book will speak to those who have read the Bible their whole lives and to those who have never heard of Jesus. Brian uses his own life lessons and adventures combined with Bible history and scripture to help us recognize how Jesus is our companion and is calling us to be bold and righteous. He shows us that submitting to Jesus is the most powerful thing any of us can do. You will complete this book feeling inspired and encouraged to know and serve Jesus more.

—Angie Dahlgren
Port Security Officer
Port of Portland, Oregon
West Linn 16U Softball Coach

As I read Brian's manuscript for this book, I understood more of the back story that caused me to respect him and appreciate him as a fellow youth pastor, a senior pastor, and a longtime friend. He has gently, without any male *chest-beating*, helped us (and not just us males) to see certain aspects of Jesus's life that can help us all to live with humility, courage, and love.

It is especially good for me, and maybe one or two of you that want to join me, in our shared failures. Not through any guilting, but in Jesus's love and acceptance for us, I can, like Peter, come back to Him again and again. You'll see Jesus's work in this guy, and all of us guys can benefit. Enjoy the read!

—Andy Gilbert
Retired Director of Young Ministries
High School Pastor
Eugene Faith Center

ACKNOWLEDGMENTS

I would like to thank the following people for making this book possible.

Jesus, for giving me the inspiration and revelation.

Wendy Buhler, thank you for your countless hours editing this project. Your suggestions were invaluable!

My wife, Robann; you mowed the lawn for me and accepted my excuse of "I have to work on my book."

Marie Lewis, thanks for all the help and encouragement.

INTRODUCTION

Many years ago, my son told me that I should write a book. At the time, it seemed like a good idea, but then I began to debate with myself about it.

What in the world would you write about, Brian? Maybe rewrite the book of James. After all, you've memorized it and have taught on it several times, or maybe, as my son suggested, the book of Proverbs.

Of course, my thoughts would attack me again. *There are plenty of books and commentaries written on these. What else could I write on? Who would read it anyway? Who would want to read anything written by me?*

Over the years, I have had this inner struggle going on about what I could write. Along with this was the conflict of enough time. I thought, *I don't have time to do this, and besides, it is way too much work.*

The resolution to this inner battle came like a wave crashing over me as Jesus gave me a topic that I think is very interesting, and I've not seen much written on it.

I grew up going to church and have been a pastor for over thirty years. I have always wondered why men in particular have a difficult time accepting Jesus as Lord and Savior.

Explore with me the possibility that men have a difficult time receiving Jesus because of the American portrayal of Him. We have no pictures of Jesus when He walked this earth over two thousand years ago, but from our earliest age, we have seen portraits of Him.

These portraits are someone's idea of what He looked like. Unfortunately, most of these paintings show a fair-skinned man, with long golden flowing locks of hair, dressed in a beautiful robe, with arms outstretched and an expression on his face like at any moment

He might burst into tears. Lately, artists have tried to modernize the portrayals of Jesus; many of these pictures show a 1970s California surfer dude.

As I follow God's calling to write this book, my hope is that you begin to see the man who Jesus was and is, instead of the image society has created.

Men need someone to look up to, and these images of the Savior don't depict a *man's man*. They don't represent someone to whom I can trust my life.

Most men have strong egos. The teachings of Christ are directly opposed to that pride, calling men to humble themselves and follow. Both humbling oneself and the following of someone are very difficult for men to do.

Also, there is a perception in the world that Christianity is for women and wimps, that following Jesus is for the weak, and Christianity is a crutch. When in reality, it is just the opposite.

Think about the primary followers of Christ when He was here on earth. Men. Fishermen, taxmen, and military men. These are the people He called to be world changers.

While this book will be primarily written for men, I know that women struggle with these issues too, so don't put down the book, ladies.

Travel around the scriptures with me, and let's explore the manly qualities Jesus possessed: strength in humility, righteousness in anger, and courage in the face of danger, to name a few.

I think when you have finished reading this book, you will view Jesus in a different light. He really was a *man's man*, and real men follow Him.

CHAPTER 1

THE FOCUS OF A MAN
THE POWER OF
RIGHTEOUS ANGER
CLEANSING THE TEMPLE

People would describe me as a *car nut*. I love my car. I take good care of my car. Correction: I take excellent care of my car. I wash it once a week. I wax it once a week. I've been known to take out the seats from the vehicle to vacuum underneath them. When I'm all done detailing my ride, I pull it into the garage and cover it with a car cover.

When I go someplace, I'm the jerk who parks the farthest away from the store and takes up two spaces, so my baby doesn't get door dings.

Needless to say, I love my car! Several years ago, this love of my car was tested, along with my love of our son and my temper.

As usual, our new Toyota van and *like-new* Toyota Celica were parked in the garage. Now I had told our young son to take his bike out the side door of the garage and not between the two cars. Of course, it's a lot faster and easier to go between the two cars and straight out of the garage through the big door than it would be to go through the little side door into the backyard and then through the gate. On this particular day, despite many warnings, Brian Jr. decided to take the shortcut.

Our little boy's handlebars had a grip missing, exposing the metal edge. That afternoon, I walked into the garage to go to the store when I noticed something that was not present earlier in the day. It was a scratch mark. The problem was that this scratch started at the front of the van and worked its way like a wave the full length of the vehicle. In most places, it was clear to the metal.

Have you ever been that mad? How mad you ask?

You know, *that mad!*

At that moment, I was learning the difference between unrighteous anger and righteous anger. Fortunately, my son was nowhere near me at this particular time. I was very unrighteous in my anger. So I took a walk. I prayed. It was a long walk.

James tells us, *"Dear brothers, don't ever forget that it is best to listen much, speak little, and not become angry; for anger doesn't make us good, as God demands that we must be"* (James 1:19–20 TLB).

Paul says, *"If you are angry, don't sin by nursing your grudge. Don't let the sun go down with you still angry—get over it quickly; for when you are angry, you give a mighty foothold to the devil"* (Ephesians 4:26–27 TLB).

The implication here is that you can be angry and not sin. This is what I mean by righteous anger. We can also be angry and sin. Which does not bring about *the righteousness of God.* Either way, we are to resolve that anger before the sun goes down so that we don't give the devil a foothold in our lives.

So is there a difference between *man's anger* and *God's anger?* Yes, Jesus created our emotions. Anger is one of His creations and therefore has a purpose.

Cleansing the temple

From Jesus's life we see an example of righteous anger in the story of the temple cleansing found in John 2:13–22:

> *Then it was time for the annual Jewish Passover celebration, and Jesus went to Jerusalem. In the Temple area he saw merchants selling cattle,*

sheep, and doves for sacrifices, and moneychangers behind their counters. Jesus made a whip from some ropes and chased them all out, and drove out the sheep and oxen, scattering the moneychangers' coins over the floor and turning over their tables! Then, going over to the men selling doves, he told them, 'Get these things out of here. Don't turn my Father's House into a market!'

Then his disciples remembered this prophecy from the Scriptures: 'Concern for God's House will be my undoing.' 'What right have you to order them out?' the Jewish leaders demanded. 'If you have this authority from God, show us a miracle to prove it.' 'All right,' Jesus replied, 'this is the miracle I will do for you: Destroy this sanctuary and in three days I will raise it up!'

'What!' they exclaimed. 'It took forty-six years to build this Temple, and you can do it in three days?' But by "this sanctuary" he meant his body. After he came back to life again, the disciples remembered his saying this and realized that what he had quoted from the Scriptures really did refer to him, and had all come true!

Early in Jesus's ministry, He had spent a few days with His mother, brothers, and disciples in Capernaum when He decided to journey to the capital city of Jerusalem. The Jewish leaders had instructed the people that once a year, during the Passover, they were to come to Jerusalem to sacrifice, to be taught by the rabbis, and to worship God. Large numbers assembled, coming from all parts of Palestine and even from distant lands. The temple courts were filled with Jewish people seeking to make their yearly sacrifices to God.

There were a few requirements for this sacrificial system and a few problems which Jesus encountered.

Along with freewill offerings used to support the temple, every Jew was required to pay yearly a one-half shekel as a *"ransom for his life"* (Exodus 30:12 NIV). These monies were to be deposited in the temple treasury.

The problem with this system started with *foreign money.* Pretty much anyone who lived outside of Jerusalem had *foreign money.* This had to be exchanged by the money changers for the coin of the sanctuary or *temple coin.*

The coin of the sanctuary was called a *temple shekel.* The priests required that all gifts collected and all taxes paid to the temple must first be exchanged for the temple shekels and paid with that coinage.

This gave the money changers a great opportunity for fraud. Extortion had grown into a disgraceful practice, which the priests didn't mind because this became a huge source of income for them.

The second fraud perpetrated on the people by the priests was within the sacrificial system. God had established specific guidelines for the sacrifices that the people were to make. (See the book of Leviticus.) One of these was that the sacrifice used for the freewill offering must be without blemish (Leviticus 22:21).

The priests established a system whereby *all* sacrifices must be inspected by a priest before sacrificing for blemishes. If a sacrifice had a blemish, which many of them would, the worshipper must buy (with temple shekels) a *preapproved* sacrifice.

The worshippers had been taught that if they didn't offer sacrifices, God's blessings would be removed from their homes, children, and fields. Of course, knowing these things, the animal dealers charged exorbitant prices for the preapproved animals.

They would share these profits with the priests and rulers and enrich themselves at the expense of the people.

The worshippers

Many sacrifices were offered during the Passover season, and therefore, sales at the temple were very large. This turned the temple courts from a place of contemplation into a noisy cattle market. There could be heard confrontational bargaining, cows mooing, doves cooing, and sheep bleating, all mingled with the clinking of coins.

A temple that was supposed to be a place of worship and prayer in the solitude of silence was invaded by an unholy uproar. The Jewish people were very proud of their temple regarding words spoken against it on the same level as words spoken against God—blasphemy. They were also extremely proud of their piety, and they were very particular about the performance of their ceremonies connected with the temple. Yet the love of money had overruled their values and they were unaware how far they had wandered from the original meaning of the service instituted by God himself.

The priests

The priests and rulers were called to be the representatives of God to the people; they should have corrected the abuses of the temple court and been compassionate toward their people, helping those who were not able to buy the required sacrifices; but greed had hardened their hearts.

Think of the people who would have come to the Passover. Some came from far distances and had expenses from their travel. Some who came were too poor to purchase a sacrifice for the Lord. The priests who were proud of their piety and claimed to be the covering of the people were without integrity, sympathy, or compassion.

Jesus

As Jesus came into the temple that day, he took in this whole scene. He saw the sacred outer court of His temple turned into a place of unholy traffic. He saw the cheating of the money changers in unfair transactions. He saw the exploitation of the poor.

Jesus saw that something must be done. The symbolism of this whole sacrificial system was to describe the Messiah who was standing in their midst. The worshippers offered their sacrifices without understanding that these were a picture of the only perfect sacrifice and that perfect sacrifice stood among them. The temple itself was a symbol of man; it needed correction, guidance. It needed Jesus.

Imagine what was going through the mind of the Savior as He beheld this scene in *His* temple: His children being cheated, His house being defiled, His system to remove sin being perverted, and His subjects being extorted.

Now notice what he does in verse 15: *"So he made a whip out of cords…"* I'm the kind of guy who asks questions like, "What kind of cords?" "Where did he get the cords?" "How long did it take him to *make* a whip?" "Did he leave the temple and come back?" "What did he do while he made the whip?"

I don't have answers to those questions, but it does lead me to ponder that He took the time to make a whip. He was angry but didn't immediately react. He made a whip. He was hurt by what He saw, but before responding, He wove cords together to make a whip. He was livid by what He witnessed, but before disciplining those in the wrong, He took time to contemplate. He made a whip!

Whip making is prayer time

We know from the life of Jesus that he prayed a lot. We also know from scripture that He thought prayer was important and that He commanded us to pray. Because of this, I like to think that while Jesus made the whip, one of the things He did was pray. Praying is a good thing to do when we are angry. While praying, we can weed through all of the different things going on in our hearts and minds and boil it down to "Why am I mad?" Oftentimes, hurt and being misunderstood drives anger. We get hurt, whether social, physical, or spiritual, and our response is anger.

Prayer helps us calm our spirit, understand the whys, and focus on what God wants. Prayer time helps dissolve the anger or turn it into righteous anger. Prayer time can help us hear from the Holy Spirit (if our anger is righteous anger) and guide us with what to do next.

Whip making is meditation time

Whip making is meditation time. The Bible tells us in Joshua 1:8 (NIV), *"Keep this Book of the Law always on your lips; meditate on it day and night, so that you may be careful to do everything written in it. Then you will be prosperous and successful."*

In the 119th chapter of Psalms, we're told to meditate on God's precepts, meditate on His decrees, meditate on His wonders, meditate on His promises, meditate on His statutes and love His law, and meditate on it all day long. Reading God's Word and meditating on Him can calm our emotions. Studying the scriptures and meditating on them helps us get God's perspective on any situation and helps us walk in the Spirit.

Whip making takes a conscious effort

Whip making takes a conscious effort. I must purposely move from a place of rage to a place of calm. Counselors tell us to count to ten or to take a walk or take a *pregnant pause*. The point of these things is to remove ourselves from responding at that particular time.

Jesus made a whip.

I took a walk.

It takes a conscious effort to find out if this is godly anger or ungodly rage.

Whip making takes time

From John's account in the scriptures, it reads as if Jesus walked into the temple, saw the sights, pulled a whip out of His pocket, and cleared the scene. When in reality, He made a whip from cords. I personally don't believe He had the cords with Him. I believe He left the temple, went and rounded up some rope or leather strands, and wove a whip together. He then came back and cleared the temple.

So you may think, "What's the big deal of how it happened?" Because whip making takes time. When we are faced with a situation that causes us to get angry, we must take time to resolve the issue. This sometimes means dealing with and forgiving a person who hurt us or correcting a situation that resulted in frustration, even dealing with an internal problem that causes anger. Whip making is a good way to ensure that our anger is righteous; another way is to forgive.

Dealing with forgiveness

The Bible speaks volumes on the subject of forgiveness:

> For if you forgive men when they sin against you, your heavenly Father will also forgive you. But if you do not forgive men their sins, your Father will not forgive your sins. (Matthew 6:14–15 NIV)

> Then Peter came to Jesus and asked, "Lord, how many times shall I forgive my brother when he sins against me? Up to seven times?" Jesus answered, "I tell you, not seven times, but seventy-seven times." (Matthew 18:21–22 NIV)

> And when ye stand praying, forgive, if ye have ought against any: that your Father also which is in heaven may forgive you your trespasses. But if ye do not forgive, neither will your Father which is in heaven forgive your trespasses. (Mark 11:25–26 KJV)

> Take heed to yourselves: If thy brother trespass against thee, rebuke him; and if he repents, forgive him. And if he trespass against thee seven times in a day, and seven times in a day turn again to thee, saying, I repent; thou shalt forgive him. (Luke 17:3–4 KJV)

Books have been written on forgiveness. One thing is certain—there is a progression that leads to death of which anger and unforgiveness are a part.

Hurt oftentimes causes anger; at this point, choices need to be made. Will we forgive, watch the anger dissipate, and be refocused to a righteous anger or harbor unforgiveness and let sinful anger grow in our lives?

If we choose not to forgive, the next step will be bitterness. Hebrews tells us, *"Make every effort to live in peace with all men and to be holy; without holiness, no one will see the Lord. See to it that no one misses the grace of God and that no bitter root grows up to cause trouble and defile many"* (Hebrews 12:14–15 NIV). If we choose not to deal with the hurt and anger, a bitter root will grow in our hearts. Soon we will become angry people. From this bitterness, we will be moved to hatred, and from there, we harbor murder in our hearts.

The root of my unrighteous anger is not letting the grace of God work in areas of my life that have been damaged. I must forgive to be healthy spiritually. If there is unforgiveness in my heart, I can be sure that my anger is not righteous.

Jesus told us in Matthew 5:23–24 (KJV), *"Therefore if thou bring thy gift to the altar, and there rememberest that thy brother hath ought against thee; Leave there thy gift before the altar, and go thy way; first be reconciled to thy brother, and then come and offer thy gift."*

We must also be right with others both by forgiving them and by making sure that they forgive us wherever possible. This also applies to our standing before God. I must make sure that sin does not have a foothold in my life by regularly repenting of my sin and asking Jesus to forgive me. If I'm not diligent in making sure my heart and spirit are clean before the Lord, then anger can work destruction in my life.

If I work through my anger, hurt, and pain and forgive myself and others, then I can see if God is focusing my anger on unrighteousness. If God chooses to give us righteous anger, then we may have more work to do. Maybe more prayer or like in Jesus's case, cleanse the temple.

Back to the temple

After making the whip, Jesus was still angry and returned to the temple focused. He had a mission and that was to cleanse His house of sin. He spoke loud and clear, His voice echoing throughout the temple courts. *"Get these out of here! How dare you turn my Father's house into a market!"*

Jesus cracked His handmade whip and drove all the animals and sellers from the temple area. He flipped over the tables of the money changers and scattered their coins. I'm sure even His disciples were scared of Jesus at that moment. Later, John would record this incident and remember his feelings at that moment and call it *zeal*. He would then quote a messianic Psalm, *"For the zeal of thine house hath eaten me up; and the reproaches of them that reproached thee are fallen upon me"* (Psalm 69:9 KJV).

My friend Bruce calls this *focus*. John called it zeal. I call it God-given, righteous anger. Some would say that it would be a sin for Jesus to get angry, and He never sinned. But I refer back to Paul saying, *"In your anger do not sin."*

Later in Jesus's ministry, there is a story in the book of Mark where Jesus got angry again:

> *Then Jesus asked them, 'Which is lawful on the Sabbath: to do good or to do evil, to save life or to kill?' But they remained silent. He looked around at them in anger and, deeply distressed at their stubborn hearts, said to the man, 'Stretch out your hand.' He stretched it out, and his hand was completely restored.* (Mark 3:4–5 NIV; italics mine)

Righteous anger

A number of times in scripture, we see Jesus moving in righteous anger. Before He cleansed the temple, He had spent forty days and forty nights in the wilderness, fasting and being tested by the devil. In that exchange, He tells Satan, *"Get out of here, Satan, the Scriptures say, 'worship only the Lord God. Obey only Him"* (Matthew 4:10 TLB).

When the woman caught in adultery was brought to Him in John 8, He confronted their sin, *"When they kept on questioning him, he straightened up and said to them, 'If any one of you is without sin, let him be the first to throw a stone at her'"* (John 8:7 NIV).

In His condemnation of the Pharisees in Matthew 23, He seems to be very angry. He called them hypocrites. He condemned them for not practicing what they preached, for tying heavy loads on the shoulders of the people while making a show of their own righteousness. He exposed the evil of their hearts, leading the people astray while mistreating the poor and widows.

These verses show us that anger is a part of who God is and give us a perfect example of what righteous anger is.

Righteous anger will always be motivated by love but will expose evil. Righteous anger is anger at injustice and the mistreatment of God's people. Righteous anger desires repentance because it hates the results of sin.

Definition of anger

Webster's Dictionary defines anger as *"a strong feeling of displeasure usually of antagonism, rage, of being upset or annoyed because of something wrong or bad; the feeling that makes someone want to hurt other people, to shout, etc."*[1]

This is a perfect definition of man's anger. Man's anger can come from different things. It can be produced by one's expectations not being met or something going against one's values. It can be produced by fear of what is happening or of what might happen. A person who feels they are being unfairly or unjustly treated might become angry.

Man's anger

There is a power to anger; that power can be destructive, or it can be a force for good. Men in particular have been given a strength that sometimes shows itself in anger. But James tells us, *"For man's anger does not bring about the righteous life that God desires"* (James 1:20 NIV). The key here are the words *man's anger*. There is a difference between man's anger and God's anger.

---

[1] www.merriam-webster.com.

Man's anger is negative anger, and it destroys while God's anger is positive and always moves us forward. Christianity gives grace for man's anger and room for righteous anger.

Sometimes it's hard to distinguish between the two. One distinguishing mark is that man's anger is selfish and accomplishes its own ends while righteous anger when displayed will always point to scripture and to Christ. Proverbs also help us with this: *"A man's wisdom makes him slow to anger; it is to his glory to overlook an offense"* (Proverbs 19:11 NIV).

This verse does not say that a man's wisdom will make him never get angry again. It says, *"slow to anger."* We will be hurt in this life and a wise man, a mature Christian, chooses to overlook the offenses. He will also be slow to get angry because he is wise and because he is mature in the Lord. Also, he is a forgiving man and a whole person.

If a man is a healthy Christian, then he can be moved by the Holy Spirit to righteous anger. This kind of anger is like that of Christ's in cleansing the temple. He will be angry at injustice. He will be angry at sin. He will be angry at Satan.

Jesus loves to use angry men. I love the song by Randy Stonehill which illustrates this. It's called "Angry Young Men."

> "He wants some angry young men, ones who can't be
> bought, Ones who will not run from a fight.
> Ones who will speak the truth whether is popular or not.
> Ones who'd give up anything to walk in His light.
> Rest assured when Jesus comes again,
> He'll be looking for some angry young men.
>
> He wants some angry young men, with fire in their eyes.
> Ones who understand what Jesus gave.

Ones who have grown weary of the world and all its lies.

Ones who won't forget they've been delivered from the grave.

He wants some angry young men, who love the Lord they serve.

Ones who'll do much more than make a speech.

Ones who'll act their faith out with a passion it deserves, 'cause if we cannot live it, tell me, who are we to preach?"[2]

Athletes use anger

My friend Bruce says, "Don't get mad, get focused." As an athlete and coach, he uses this to motivate himself and his players. What he means by this is anger can be positive or negative. Anyone who has watched professional athletics has seen the positive effects of anger as well as the negative effects.

Positive anger or, as Bruce puts it, *focus*, can motivate the athlete to try harder, to refocus, and even to give them more power or endurance while negative anger can cause the athlete to lose their focus, cause them to try too hard, or just give up.

A little boy learns a lesson

A Christian man has been given a specific emotional makeup by God. There is a design in it, and it is for a purpose. By Jesus's example, much prayer, and by walking in the power of the Holy Spirit, a man can use his anger for righteousness. A godly father must walk in righteous anger many times in his life as he raises his children.

---

[2] "Angry Young Men" by Randy Stonehill in *Love Beyond Reason*, Myrrh Records, January 1, 1985.

There is a fine line between man's anger and righteous anger, but by the direction of the Holy Spirit, I can begin to discern the difference.

There is great power in a godly man moving in righteous anger. Jesus uses angry men to deal with injustice, who speak the truth in love and change the world.

By the time I got home that fateful day I was still mad, but now it was righteous anger. I found Brian and walked him the full length of the car showing him the scratch he had made. Halfway through, he began to cry. I don't know what was going through the eight-year-old's mind at the time; maybe that he was never going to see his ninth birthday. I took it as repentance.

We had a good conversation about obedience and that Daddy knows best. He was grounded from bike riding for a week, and Daddy learned a valuable lesson about the difference between punishment given through man's unrighteous anger and discipline given through God's righteous anger.

I then called my insurance agent.

CHAPTER 2

THE LOVE OF A MAN
"PETER, DO YOU LOVE ME?"

L ibby was a beautiful five-foot-one-inch-tall brunette, a mirror image of her mother. She had big brown eyes like her father (who had come over to New York from the old country of Sicily).

Libby was born in 1939; by her seventeenth birthday, she had graduated from high school and was looking forward to a bright future.

One small problem: she was pregnant. No one could know. Mama maybe, but definitely not Papa. He might kill her—literally! She was sincerely afraid. Decisions like these are never easy and especially with no one to turn to.

Papa was in the construction business, and no one ever questioned why he never carried a ruler or a hammer. After all, he was the owner of the company, so he employed people to carry the tools, make the bids, and pound the nails. People like Tony.

After dropping out of high school his senior year, Tony had gone to work for Papa. He didn't mind the work, but he would rather play his trumpet and visit with Libby.

Could she tell Tony he was going to be a father? No! He might say something stupid like *marriage*, or worse—*abortion*.

15

The power of love

In the song "Power of Love" by Huey Lewis and the News, the first verse says:

"The power of love is a curious thing
Make a one man weep, make another man sing
Change a hawk to a little white dove
More than a feeling, that's the power of love."[1]

I've often witnessed this as I've seen friends of mine fall in love. Of course, this doesn't represent all men, but I've seen enough of them go down this road causing me to believe it's the majority.

It goes something like this: A man falls in love, his wardrobe begins to change, his priority list shuffles, and new things that just happen to be his newfound love's priorities now find their way to the top of his list. Old friends are seen less and new favorite things to do are added. These new things seem to be her favorite things to do (like romantic movies). Sappy phone calls begin to happen; cards and even poems make their way into his lifestyle.

Soon he's seen wearing matching outfits with his steady. Even matching sweaters!

Fast forward—engagement, marriage, two kids. Where is this lovesick human now? Sitting on the couch in his underwear watching football and giving an occasional grunt to the love of his life.

Trouble with love relationships

I think men have trouble with balance when it comes to love. Why? Don't ask me. I don't know, but I think this is why men have trouble in a love relationship with Jesus.

---

[1] http://www.lyrics freak.com (2014).

They get confused. Are they supposed to wear a sappy Jesus sweater or sit in the back row at church on Sundays, nodding off during the sermon?

The Bible says, *"Love the Lord your God with all your heart and with all your soul and with all your mind"* (Matthew 22:37 NIV).

Men seem to have a problem understanding what this means.

Peter struggles with love

Peter seems to have struggled with this very issue. Remember at the Last Supper, he vowed to die with Jesus. Hours later in the garden of Gethsemane, he even defended Jesus with the sword. But when Jesus was arrested, he ran and hid. The next day, he even denied knowing Jesus three times.

We pick up the story sometime after the death and resurrection of Jesus. In John 21:1–23, the disciples have gone back to fishing. They have fished all night and caught nothing. Jesus showed up on the shore and asked them if they've caught anything.

"No!" came their frustrated answer, so He instructed them to cast their nets on the *"right side of the boat and you will find some. When they did, they were unable to haul the net in because of the large number of fish"* (verse 6 NIV).

At this point, they recognized that it was Jesus. Peter jumped out of the boat and swam to shore to find Jesus around *"a fire of burning coals there with fish on it, and some bread. Jesus said to them, 'Bring some of the fish you have just caught'"* (verses 9–10 NIV).

Peter was confused about his relationship with Jesus and what his future would be like now that Jesus had died and risen from the dead. So he had gone back to fishing. Back to the old life. Back to the familiar. Oftentimes, when men are confused about a relationship, they go back to the familiar.

A confrontation of love

There are only three places in the New Testament where a specific *coal* fire is mentioned. The first is in John 18:17–18 (KJV):

"Then saith the damsel that kept the door unto Peter, Art not thou also one of this man's disciples? He saith, I am not. And the servants and officers stood there, who had made a fire of coals; for it was cold: and they warmed themselves: and Peter stood with them, and warmed himself."

Peter was warming himself around a *coal* fire, and a servant girl asked if he was a disciple; he denied Jesus. The next place is here in John 21:9. Jesus built a *coal* fire to cook the fish. The third place is in Romans 12:20 (NIV): *"On the contrary: 'If your enemy is hungry, feed him; if he is thirsty, give him something to drink. In doing this, you will heap burning coals on his head.'"*

When Jesus built a coal fire, I believe it was a confrontation of love. Jesus was confronting Peter. This was a gentle reminder to Peter that he had placed himself as an enemy of Jesus by first denying knowing Jesus three times and then going back to the old way of life. Back to fishing. Jesus was reminding Peter of how far he had fallen away in his relationship with Him.

Jesus also repeated the miracle of the great catch, one of His early miracles with the disciples and Peter's first confession of Jesus as Lord. Peter had forgotten that he had committed his life to Jesus and went back to doing things his way.

Most people when talking about the love of Jesus don't like to think of how many times His love was confrontational. This is how the Lord began His reinstatement of Peter.

Love reinstates Peter

When they had finished eating, Jesus said to Simon Peter, "Simon son of John, do you truly love me more than these?" "Yes, Lord," he said, "you know that I love you." Jesus said, "Feed my lambs." Again Jesus said, "Simon son of John, do you truly love me?" He answered, "Yes, Lord, you know that I love you." Jesus said, "Take care of my sheep." The third time he said to him, "Simon son of John, do you love me?" Peter was hurt because Jesus asked him the third time, "Do you love me?" He said, "Lord,

*you know all things; you know that I love you." Jesus
said, "Feed my sheep." (John 21:15–17 NIV)*

The Greek word Jesus uses for *love* here is *agapao*. It is a derivative of the word *agape*, which is God's perfect love. *"It expresses the deep and constant love and interest of a perfect Being towards entirely unworthy objects."*[2] He was asking Peter if he dearly loved Him. If he loved Him with a committed kind of love.

When we connect it to the comment *"More than these,"* I believe Jesus was pointing to the fish. "Peter, do you love me more than your old way of life? More than your occupation? Do you love me more than anything else?"

Peter answered, *"You know I love you."* But the word Peter used for love here is *phileo*, which is brotherly love and means "to be fond of, to like, to approve of, to treat affectionately or kindly, to welcome, befriend."[3]

Then, *"Feed my lambs..."* Words are not enough; there is a mission before Peter and before us. New converts are to be cared for. Lambs (or young Christians) are to be fed.

To feed is the duty of a Christian teacher to encourage the spiritual growth of the members of the church.

Again, Jesus asked Peter if he loved Him *(agapao)*. Peter's response was *"You know I love you (phileo)."*

The command was *"Take care of my sheep."* Why a different command? According to Vine:

> *The Lord, when addressing Peter, first uses
> 'bosko' which means to nourish, then uses 'poimaino'
> which means to act as a shepherd, to 'tend.' Then He
> returns to 'bosko.' These are not simply interchangeable... Spiritual care of God's children, the feeding
> of the flock from the Word of God is a constant and*

---

[2] W. E. Vine, M.A., *Vines Expository Dictionary of New Testament Words* (McLean, Virginia: McDonald Publishing Company), 702–704.

[3] James Strong, *Strong's Exhaustive Concordance of the Bible* (McLean, Virginia: S.T.D., LL.D., McDonald Publishing Company), 75.

regular necessity. The tending consists of other acts, of discipline, authority, restoration, and material assistance of individuals. [4]

Now Jesus asked Peter a third time if he loved Him. Only this time, He used the word *phileo*. This would be like Jesus saying, "Peter, do you even like me? Are you even my friend?"

Peter must now search his deepest feelings. He must be honest with God. *"Lord you know all things."*

Jesus was issuing a command to Peter, and to us, to shepherd his sheep. To care for their spiritual needs.

Sheep would mean all of God's people. To feed the young ones, to discipline the stubborn ones, and to tenderly watch over the mature ones.

This is the power of love. This is the kind of love Jesus has for all of us. It is a strong love. It is confrontational. Because of Jesus's love for Peter, He wouldn't leave him in his sin. He wouldn't let him continue to wander. He gave him a purpose.

Peter figured out what a long and loving relationship really was. He came to understand the kind of love Jesus has for His followers.

In the first five chapters of the book of Acts, we see the impact of his changed life. Peter's life changed dramatically in Acts 2 when he was baptized with the Holy Spirit and preached to thousands of people, of which three thousand were saved.

He also experienced the power of love, as love transformed his life from a loud, impetuous, and fearful follower to one who was hung upside down on a cross because he felt unworthy to be crucified in the same manner as his Lord and Savior Jesus.[5]

That's the power of love.

We see Peter's love changed because of what he had experienced in his walk with Christ. Here are some of the principles he learned and what we can glean from his life lessons.

---

[4] Vine, *Vines Expository Dictionary*, 427–428.

[5] John Foxe, "Chapter 1," in *Foxe's Book of Martyrs*, www.sacred-texts.com/chr/martyrs/fox101.htm.

Changed by love

1. *Love starts with humility.*

   The first principle is that love starts with humility. Peter was sensitive, and he had a tender conscience. He knew his own heart. He knew he had failed Jesus and now gone back to his old ways, but he was humble enough to repent. This is what starts to mature his love. He knew his shortcomings because he knew himself.

   We see that men often start a relationship in great humility. (Remember the matching sweaters?) This humility must remain if our love is to mature. In a relationship, whether it be with Jesus or others, we must be willing to admit when we are wrong. We also must repent of that sin and ask forgiveness. Forgiving ourselves and others takes humility but is essential. It takes humility to do these things and that humility is what starts love on the pathway to greatness. Jesus gives grace to the humble (Proverbs 3:34).

2. *Love is forged by failure.*

   A storm at sea. A ghost walking on the water. A voice called out to the apostles, *"Take heart! It is I, do not be afraid."*

   "'Lord, if it's you,' Peter replied, 'tell me to come to you on the water.'"

   The Lord said, *"Come,"* and Peter jumped over the side of the boat.

   Suddenly he awakened to what he was doing. Walking on the water! This does not make any sense, and in his fear, he started to sink.

   "Lord save me!" Peter cried out and Jesus was there to lift him up and put him back aboard the ship (Matthew 14:27–30).

   Peter's life is riddled with failure, but love is forged by failure. That is another reason why Peter's love grew so strong. He failed all the time. Jesus said, *"Therefore, I tell you, her many sins have been forgiven—for she loved much. But he who has been forgiven little loves little"* (Luke 7:47 NIV).

If we fail a lot, we are forgiven a lot; if we are forgiven a lot, we love a lot.

We seem to always learn more from our defeats than from our successes. I think this is because we often enjoy success and don't look for the reason behind the victory. But when defeat, failure, and pain are involved, we almost always ask a simple question: *"Why?"*

When we ask that question, we make room for learning and growth. Relationships always involve failure. Peter's sure did. When we make room for failure by embracing it when it happens, learning from it, growing by it, and forgiving ourselves and others, then like Peter, our love will be strengthened.

3. *Love matures by death.*

That night in the temple courts, recorded in Mark 14:67–72, Peter is confronted at least three times. First, standing around a coal fire, he is confronted by a servant girl.

"You were there too. You were with this man from Nazareth, this Jesus."

"You're mistaken, I don't know what you're talking about," is Peter's quick response.

But then another girl came to where he stood and turned to him. "He is one of them," she said.

Peter talked a little louder than before, and now they could all hear him as he denied Jesus a second time.

This one, who at the supper just the night before promised he would never deny Jesus; in fact, he would be willing to die for Him and die he did.

Then a soldier joined the group. Perhaps one of the death squads who will crucify Jesus in just a few hours or one of the soldiers who had arrested Jesus in the garden of Gethsemane.

"He is one of them."

And someone else said, "Surely you are one of them. You must be. I can tell by your accent, you are a Galilean."

At that point Peter began to swear, possibly using language he has not used in years, and shouted, "I do not know this man you speak of!"

In that quiet moment, he could hear it, loud and clear, the crowing of the cock! And he remembered, *"Before the cock crows twice, you will disown me three times."*

At that very moment, the Lord appeared and looked directly into Peter's eyes. It was more than Peter could take; out into the night, he ran and wept, and a little bit of Peter died.

Love was beginning to mature as Peter died from his selfishness. His self-reliance had taken a fatal blow.

Love matures by death. In order for love to mature, self must die. Self-centeredness, selfishness, and self-reliance must be crucified.

Peter later put it this way: *"He himself bore our sins in his body on the tree, so that we might die to sins and live for righteousness; by his wounds, you have been healed"* (1 Peter 2:24 NIV).

Like Peter, we men in particular struggle with this because we are the providers, we are the head of the home, the strong ones. Self-reliance is difficult to relinquish, but it must die, so Christ can be the Lord of our lives.

4. *Love must have a purpose.*

Finally, back to that morning by the sea of Galilee, Jesus gave the command, *"Feed my sheep,"* and Peter was sent back to Jerusalem, back to the place where he had failed Jesus. He had a purpose now—to shepherd the people of God's pasture. To preach, teach, and disciple all who would receive Jesus.

Love must have a purpose.

I'll call Maria! Libby thought. *I'll tell her I would like to visit her in California.*

Maria, Libby's sister, had married a navy man who was stationed in San Diego.

After two months in navy housing with Maria, Libby began to *show* a little. She had gotten a job at the Rexall Drugstore in Pacific Beach and worked with a wonderful mother of three boys named Lettie.

She could trust Lettie, so one day at work, Libby wept while for the first time in over four months, she had spoken to anyone of her dilemma. She had already decided on her own to have the baby but not to keep it. The baby must be put up for adoption.

"I'm so confused and lost. I don't know what to do," she cried.

Without missing a beat Lettie responded, *"Come live with us till the birth of the baby! My sister can't have children. Dorothy and Jack have already adopted a baby girl six years ago and would love to have another child. She is a great mother, and I'll help take care of everything."*

Three months later, a five-pound baby boy was born (over a month premature). Libby couldn't bear to hold him as he was taken by ambulance from Mercy Hospital to Sharpe's Children's Hospital.

After a month in an incubator, Jack and Dorothy named their new son Brian. Libby was already back in New York. This little baby would be told from birth that he was a special gift from God because they got to choose him.

This is a story of love. This is the story of adoption. This is my story. While I don't know many of the facts surrounding my adoption, this is how I imagined it happened.

The main point is the power of love. Love was shown to me by Libby who chose life though it would have been much easier to abort. Love was shown by Aunt Lettie and Uncle Bert to allow Libby to move into their crowded home, care for her like a daughter, and arrange the adoption. Love was shown by Jack and Dorothy who raised me, taught me, provided for me, and always let me know how much they loved me.

Jesus desires to adopt all of us into His family. He chose us. He sacrificed His life, so we could love Him.

There is saving power in love.

CHAPTER 3

THE STRENGTH OF A MAN
THE POWER OF
PHYSICAL STRENGTH

When I was in junior high school, I was short. Okay, I'm still short; but I mean really short, like four feet seven inches in the ninth grade. On my first day of junior high, I was walking to my very first class, and I passed two giant ninth graders. They were at least five feet seven inches tall. Looking down at me, one turned to the other and said, "They're getting smaller every year!" That was the beginning of the worst three years of my life.

Junior high is a rough time of life, but being short in junior high is awful. I got picked on. A lot. In fact (and I don't think I have a short-person complex), being short is hard our entire lives.

America reveres tall people. At least it's that way for males. Think of it. Aren't most athletes tall? Aren't most movie stars tall? Society has always favored the tall, dark and handsome man.

While height is one physical aspect of importance to the male, another is strength. Strength is important to men whether it be the physical strength of the athlete, the prowess of the soldier, or the power of a car engine.

To the male, might matters even if it's not physical, muscular strength. It could be intelligence, wit, or wisdom. As long as he feels powerful.

This is one reason why following Jesus is so difficult for a man. It is the perception, though false, that Christianity is for the little old lady. Of course, we all know the *church lady* you know; mentally weak but judgmentally strong. Unfortunately, Christianity has been portrayed as a religion for the weak and needy.

A look at the life of Jesus will quickly dispel this myth. In this chapter we will study three stories, though there are many more, where the physical, mental, and spiritual prowess of Jesus is highlighted.

In the temple

In the Jewish culture, the completion of the twelfth year was the point where a Hebrew boy became a man. He would now be called a *son of the law* and a *son of God.* New opportunities opened up for him to study the Torah and to participate in the sacred feasts and observances.

Joseph and Mary went to Jerusalem every year to celebrate the Passover, and when Jesus was of the required age, they took Him with them. This was Jesus's first Passover visit to the Holy City.

After the feast, Joseph and Mary left Jerusalem in a large caravan to return to their home in Galilee. In the confusion and the pleasure of traveling with friends, they didn't notice Jesus's absence until the evening when they stopped their travel for the night. They worriedly returned to Jerusalem and frantically searched for their Son. Finally, after three unbelievable days, they found Him in the temple, in the school of the rabbis. They had very mixed emotions upon finding Him. Joyful that He was found but angry that He would do this to them:

> When his parents saw him, they were aston-
> ished. His mother said to him, 'Son, why have you
> treated us like this? Your father and I have been
> anxiously searching for you." Why were you search-

27

ing for me?' he asked. 'Didn't you know I had to be in my Father's house?' But they did not understand what he was saying to them. (Luke 2:48–50 NIV)

Jesus teaches the teachers

"After three days they found him in the temple courts, sitting among the teachers, listening to them and asking them questions. Everyone who heard him was amazed at his understanding and his answers" (Luke 2:46–47 NIV).

That day in the sacred school, Jesus sat at the feet of the learned rabbis. He listened to their instruction and asked them questions. The scripture says that everyone was amazed at His wisdom.

Jesus must have discussed the prophecies concerning the Messiah. He impressed these scholars with His understanding of the deep truths and hidden mysteries found in the scriptures.

As a twelve-year-old, Jesus impressed learned men and His parents with His intelligence, wisdom, and deep understanding of the Torah. As an adolescent, Jesus was smart yet humble. Strong but He also listened and asked questions. This was a perfect example of meekness, power under control.

He lived a balanced life

He was already an impressive and intelligent young man at age twelve but verse 52 (NIV) says, *"And Jesus grew in wisdom and stature, and in favor with God and men."* Jesus increased in wisdom; that was mental growth. He increased in stature, which was physical growth. He also grew in favor with God and man; that is spiritually and socially strong.

He lived a balanced life. And we, too, must work on the whole person. Always learning, studying, growing in wisdom. We should keep ourselves in good physical shape because this sharpens our mind and spirit as well. We should strive to continue to grow in our relationship with Jesus and love others.

Jesus showed that Christianity is not for the weak-minded or fainthearted; it takes wisdom and strength.

In the wilderness

In Matthew 4:1–11, we have the story of the temptation of Jesus by Satan in the wilderness. *"Then Jesus was led by the Spirit into the desert to be tempted by the devil. After fasting forty days and forty nights, he was hungry"* (Matthew 4:1–2 NIV).

When I was a young man, I fasted for twenty-one days. My fast consisted of fruit juices only. It was a wonderful experience, both physically and spiritually. I learned a lot about myself, commitment, and discipline. I have since only done that one other time. The reason for this is that it was really hard. I can only imagine how much more difficult it would be to drink only water, and as in the case of Jesus, to extend that to forty days.

Jesus had just been baptized by John the Baptist in the Jordan River. The Spirit had descended on Him to anoint Him for His ministry to come, and God the Father had spoken His approval from heaven. Immediately the Spirit led Jesus to the wilderness. For every high, there must come a low. For every mountaintop, there comes a wilderness. It seems to be the law of life.

We would do well to learn this lesson from the Word; when life has brought us to the mountaintop, we need to be on our guard because this is when we are in the greatest danger of the wilderness. Think about these spiritual mountaintops: salvation, baptism, retreats, being specially used by Jesus, just to name a few. After these times, we must be very cautious of a wilderness experience just around the corner.

And that's exactly where Jesus was led—*to the wilderness*. It took place near the Dead Sea. Even today, there is a wilderness near there that covers about thirty-five miles.

Jesus went into that wilderness to be alone. Sometimes it's good for us to be alone. It was a time of contemplation, a time of prayer, a time alone with God. There are certain things which we have to work out alone.

Going through the wilderness is God's will for us. Look at the many examples in scripture:

1. Joseph was thrown into a pit and sold into slavery in Egypt.
2. Moses ran to Midian to be a shepherd for forty years.
3. David was in the wilderness three different times, first as a shepherd boy, then Saul chased him there to kill him. Finally, his son Absalom took over his kingdom, and David was forced to run to the wilderness once again.
4. Elijah was commanded by God to go to the wilderness where he was fed by ravens.
5. Paul was in prison
6. John was exiled to the isle of Patmos.

Be prepared but embrace the wilderness. It is Jesus's training field. The wilderness can be taxing both physically and spiritually. Jesus camped for forty days with a water supply and the clothes on His back.

It takes a strong man to do that!

In the presence of evil

> And when the tempter came to him, he said, 'If thou be the Son of God, command that these stones be made bread.' But he answered and said, 'It is written, Man shall not live by bread alone, but by every word that proceedeth out of the mouth of God.'
>
> Then the devil taketh him up into the holy city, and setteth him on a pinnacle of the temple, and saith unto him, 'If thou be the Son of God, cast thyself down: for it is written, He shall give his angels charge concerning thee: and in their hands they shall bear thee up, lest at any time thou dash thy foot against a stone.' Jesus said unto him, 'It is

written again, Thou shalt not tempt the Lord thy God.'

Again, the devil taketh him up into an exceeding high mountain, and sheweth him all the kingdoms of the world, and the glory of them; And saith unto him, 'all these things will I give thee, if thou wilt fall down and worship me.' Then saith Jesus unto him, 'Get thee hence, Satan: for it is written, Thou shalt worship the Lord thy God, and him only shalt thou serve.' Then the devil leaveth him, and, behold, angels came and ministered unto him. (Matthew 4:3–11 KJV)

Lust of the flesh (body)

The tempter launched his attack against Jesus along three lines. They were the same three lines he used in the garden with Adam and Eve.

First, there was the temptation to turn the stones into bread. The desert was littered with little round pieces of limestone rock which were exactly like little loaves; even they would suggest this temptation to Jesus.

This was the *lust of the flesh*. It attacks the natural cravings of the physical body. As in Genesis 3:6 (NIV), *"Eve saw that the tree was good for food."* In the same way, Jesus saw that the stones could be good for food to satisfy His hunger.

It was a temptation to Jesus to use His powers selfishly and for His own benefit. That is precisely what Jesus would always refuse to do. There is always the temptation to use selfishly whatever powers God has given to us. Again, the lust of the flesh. It is a temptation to please the body; to use our gifts, resources, and powers for the comfort and pleasure of our bodies.

All of us will be tempted to use our gifts selfishly.

So Jesus answered the tempter in the very words that express the lesson which God had sought to teach His people in the wilderness:

"Man does not live by bread alone, but that man lives by everything that proceeds out of the mouth of God."

The only way to true strength is the way which has learned complete dependence on God.

Pride of life (soul)

So Satan renewed his attack from another angle. He took Jesus to the pinnacle of the temple. Wouldn't people be so impressed by a person, a superman, who could leap off the temple and land unharmed, that they would follow him? Wasn't there a promise that the angels would hold God's man in their hands so no harm should come to him? (Psalm 91:11–12). Jesus could have said, "That's right, Satan. I'll show you that the scriptures are true and that I'm the Son of God. I'll prove to you how powerful I really am."

Lucifer's second temptation dealt with the pride of life. Just like Eve saw that *"the tree was to be desired to make one wise,"* there is a desire in every one of us to be right and to prove others wrong. Pride of life encourages us to show off just how strong we are. Jesus would not let pride rule His decisions; He would not let His pride prove the devil wrong.

"You shall not put the Lord your God to a test," Jesus said.

He meant this: there is no good in putting yourself deliberately into a threatening situation and doing it quite recklessly and needlessly, and then expecting God to rescue you from it.

Jesus expects us to take risks in order to be true to Him, but He does not expect us to take risks to enhance our own prestige.

Lust of the eye (spirit)

Then came his third and final attack.

It was the world that Jesus came to save.

So the tempting voice said, *"Fall down and worship me, and I will give you all the kingdoms of this world."*

The third temptation was the lust of the eye. *"Eve saw that the tree was pleasant to the eyes."* This is really a temptation to the spirit.

Satan was commanding Jesus to compromise. Come to terms with the world; be politically correct instead of presenting God's commands to it. It was the temptation to compromise His values just a little to reach the world. To try to change the world by becoming like it.

Back came Jesus's answer. *"You shall fear the Lord your God; You shall serve Him and swear by His Name"* (Deuteronomy 6:13 NIV).

Jesus was quite certain that we can never defeat evil by compromising with evil.

On display in this story is Jesus's incredible strength mentally, physically, and spiritually. He had made His decisions concerning the temptations. He would never entice men into following Him. There would be no compromise in His message or in the faith He demanded. This choice would inevitably lead to the cross.

We must avoid the temptation to use our gifts, talents, and resources for our own personal gain. We must not offer a Christianity that entices people to follow because of what they can get out of it. It is not a prosperity doctrine; on the contrary, it is a doctrine of giving all we have to reach others, of taking up the cross and following him.

We must not water down the gospel. We must never compromise with the world or the devil. We must live by the whole gospel, from Old Testament to New Testament.

In the hold of hate

"Then Pilate took Jesus and had him flogged. The soldiers twisted together a crown of thorns and put it on his head. They clothed him in a purple robe" (John 19:1–2 NIV).

When Jesus was arrested, He was brought before Pilate, the Roman governor. This trial took place at Pilate's palace: the praetorium. Pilate ordered that Jesus be whipped, so He was taken into the basement of the palace. The Roman scourging of forty lashes minus one was gruesome and torturous.

The soldiers would have removed Jesus's clothes and tied Him to a whipping post. Then they beat Him with a whip called a *cat-o'-nine-tails,* which consisted of nine straps of leather with a ball of leather at the end of each strap. Stuck in the ball of leather were bits of bone, iron, and chain to make the whip heavy and sharp. It was not uncommon for a person receiving a Roman scourging to die from it.

When the whip struck His back, each strand of leather would go in different directions cutting, tearing, and ripping Christ's flesh. The Bible tells us that Jesus was beaten beyond recognition *"as a man."*

The game of the kings

> *Then Pilate released Barabbas to them. And after he had whipped Jesus, he gave him to the Roman soldiers to take away and crucify. But first they took him into the armory and called out the entire contingent. They stripped him and put a scarlet robe on him, and made a crown from long thorns and put it on his head, and placed a stick in his right hand as a scepter and knelt before him in mockery. 'Hail, King of the Jews,' they yelled. And they spat on him and grabbed the stick and beat him on the head with it. After the mockery, they took off the robe and put his own garment on him again, and took him out to crucify him.* (Matthew 27:26–31 TLB)

Years ago, I had the privilege of going on a tour of Israel. One day, we were taken to the basement of the praetorium. The guide showed us carvings in the sandstone tiles of the floor and told us this history of the torture of Jesus.

They played a game with Jesus called the *game of the kings*. The steps of this game are still engraved on the stone floor. This game was outlawed because it usually resulted in the prisoner's death, but special permission was given at times for those prisoners who were condemned to death.

They would roll goat's knuckles and then move the prisoner around the game board and at each *square* or step, they would abuse him. Needless to say, the scene in the praetorium was not very pretty; apparently in Jesus's case, according to the scriptures, the first step was stripping Him.

The soldiers stripped Jesus of His own clothes and put a purple robe and a red cape on Him. Evidently, they had Him sit down on some sort of chair, where they gave Him a stick to hold so that He would look kinglier. One by one, the soldiers approached Jesus and knelt down before Him, pretending to worship Him. Then they stood up and in utter contempt spat on Jesus, took the stick out of His hand, and hit Him on the head with it. They then drove a crown of thorns deep into Jesus's skull. Soon His face was covered with spit and blood. Finally, they put Jesus's own clothes back on Him and led Him from the praetorium to crucify Him.

On the cross

"Carrying his own cross, he went out to the place of the Skull (which in Aramaic is called Golgotha)" (John 19:17 NIV). Having a prisoner who was condemned to death by crucifixion carry his cross was a common Roman custom. It wasn't the whole cross that they carried but the crossbeam called a *patibulum*. It probably weighed over forty pounds.

"Here they crucified him, and with him two others—one on each side and Jesus in the middle" (John 19:18 NIV). The Romans were very skilled at crucifixion. Jesus's hands were nailed to the cross as the soldiers found the spot on the wrist where the two bones come together. Being careful not to hit the main artery, they drove the iron spikes through Jesus's wrists into the wood.

Next came the feet. They made sure that the knees were bent so that the dying man could stretch up to get air to breathe, otherwise they would die of suffocation too quickly. One spike was driven through both ankles. The condemned was hoisted into the air to die slowly and painfully.

A strong man

Jesus was a strong man physically. Only a person in incredible shape could endure the persecution Jesus went through. The beating alone killed many prisoners. The *game of the kings* also killed an average prisoner. After these two events, Jesus carried His cross and then hung on that cross for three hours.

Life lessons

What are some things we can learn from Jesus's strength?

In the book of Matthew, Jesus said, *"I tell you the truth…"* thirty-one times. When Jesus stood before Pilate, he said, *"You are right in saying I am a king. In fact, for this reason, I was born, and for this I came into the world, to testify to the truth. Everyone on the side of truth listens to me"* (John 18:37 NIV). Jesus told the truth, taught the truth, and testified to the truth.

And *"what is truth? Pilate asked"* (John 18:38 NIV).

"I am the way and the truth and the life. No one comes to the Father except through me. Jesus answered" (John 14:6 NIV).

There is absolute truth. Jesus is the *truth*, and He teaches us the truth. In a society that values personal opinion over the truth, we must continue to study the Bible, the unchanging, infallible Word of God.

"Study to shew thyself approved unto God, a workman that needeth not to be ashamed, rightly dividing the word of truth" (2 Timothy 2:15 KJV).

Jesus told us in Matthew 10:38 (NIV), *"Anyone who does not take his cross and follow me is not worthy of me."*

Letting us know Christianity is for the strong. It takes strength, commitment, discipline, hard work, study, focus, and faith to follow Jesus.

While Christianity is also for the weak, we are reminded that with Christ in our weakness, we are still strong. The Word tells us when we are weak then He is strong (2 Corinthians 12:10) and in

Mark 14:38 (NIV) that we should *"watch and pray so that you will not fall into temptation. The spirit is willing, but the body is weak."*

Jesus did all this so that when we are lonely, we have a friend. When we are lost, He will find us. When we are mistreated, we have One who understands. When we are confused, He shows us the way. When we are sick, we can be healed.

"Who his own self bore our sins in his own body on the tree, that we, being dead to sins, should live unto righteousness: by whose stripes ye were healed" (1 Peter 2:24 KJV).

In other words, we are strong because he is strong with us and for us.

[1] Dawson McAllister, *A Walk with Christ to the Cross* (Dallas, Texas: Roper Press, 1980).

[2] Bill O'Reilly and Martin Dugard, *Killing Jesus* (Henry Holt and Company LLC, 2013).

CHAPTER 4

THE STRUGGLES OF A MAN
"A FOLLOWER OF JESUS"

Precise timing was everything when diving off The Clam, and oh, was my timing off!

It was another beautiful August day in San Diego. The weather didn't change much in my hometown, but summer was always the best. So what does a sixteen-year-old California boy do on another seventy-five-degree summer vacation day? Hang out with his cousins and go to the beach, of course.

Danny and I were more than cousins; we were best friends. His blond hair, his extra year of life, and his five inches more of height, I looked up to Danny. Literally. We had fun together, no matter what we did. And, well, teenagers don't always make good decisions—we were no exceptions.

"Let's go dive off The Clam!" I suggested.

In La Jolla, there was a cliff above the ocean called The Clam. It was named this because the ledge that jutted out on the top of a cave was shaped like a clamshell.

The goal was to dive from the clamshell down to the water thirty feet below. The target was at the mouth of a cave about eight feet deep with barnacle-covered rocks on the bottom. Trying to time the dive to hit the water when a swell came in, then breaking the dive quickly enough upon entering the water to not dive too deeply, was vitally important.

"And let's talk like English guys," Danny interjected.

When we arrived, Danny added, "We need to be nonchalant, talking in the accent quietly to each other, so it's not too obvious."

This was a great plan. We parked his blue 1963 Ford Falcon and walked past the shell shop, down the cliffs to where the infamous Clam was. Just a few weeks prior, Danny and I had been featured in an article about The Clam in the Sierra Mesa Sentinel newspaper. Pictures and everything! Needless to say, we were two young men who were pretty full of ourselves when it came to cliff diving.

The cliffs were crowded with young people. Most were watching the brave souls jumping from the ledge. We mingled among the crowd, talking quietly in our famed English accents just loud enough for people to hear.

"Look over 'ere, Daniel, it's beautiful!" I commented. As our conversation continued, people began to notice that there may be a couple of strangers here among the faithful Clam dwellers.

Time to set the hook and reel them in.

"Look 'ow 'igh this is, Daniel!" I exclaimed standing on one side of the cliff.

"Are you guys from around here?" a skinny kid asked.

"No," we answered in unison. "Do people really jump off this thing?"

"Oh, yes!" the nerdy kid answered.

"Watch meeeee!"

In midsentence, he ran and launched himself off the sandstone clam-shaped ledge and landed feet first in the water, completely thrilled with himself.

As we stood there acting as if we were shocked and totally amazed at what had just transpired, a beautiful blonde beach babe engaged us in conversation. Our plan was working better than we could have imagined.

"Where are you guys from?" she asked.

"England." Again, answering in unison.

"Oh, what part?"

"Wales," Danny quickly responded. Of course, neither of us knew anything about England except that it was where The Beatles came from.

"How long are you staying in California?" she inquired.

"Oh, about two months," Danny replied, always quicker on the draw than me, especially when it came to talking to girls.

"Have you ever been here before?" she continued, as the boy who had just jumped returned to where we were standing.

After landing in the water at The Clam, the jumper would have to swim over to the left side of the cave opening. It took experience to know that the easiest way to climb back up was to wait for a swell to come in. It would lift you up and with a couple of swimming strokes, it was actually possible to land standing up on the big rock that was the first exit step. Then it was a short climb up the side of the cliff. Handholds and footholds were well-worn into the rock, so it only took a few minutes to climb back up.

However, not waiting for a swell made it almost impossible to try to climb up a barnacled-covered rock. A person trying to climb up from there or one who missed the landing when the swell came in could be spun around the rocks. It would be like being in a washing machine before being spit out to sea. We had watched this happen to tourists many times over the years.

"Why don't you try it?" the skinny kid questioned, jumping right in the middle of our conversation.

"Oh, I don't think so!" I responded.

"I'll do it if you will," Danny replied.

Amid much chatter and excitement about the English guys going to jump off The Clam, I stepped out onto the ledge. Moving slowly to the edge and looking down, I exclaimed, "Oh, no! It's a long way down."

My voice trembled as my acting skills improved. "Well, as we say in England, 'ere goes nutin'," and off I flew with a profession-al-looking swan dive. Popping up from below I shouted, "Com' on down, Daniel, the water's fine!"

Danny quickly stepped up and launched into a *full gainer* (which was a leap forward and then a full backflip landing feet first in the water). Dan just happened to be a high school gymnast.

As we climbed back up to the top, the mood had drastically changed. All of a sudden, people weren't fascinated with us. They were actually mad at us!

"You've been here before," the skinny kid barked.

"No, but we do a li'le divin' in England," Dan calmly answered.

"You're experts!" someone shouted.

"Do it again!"

"Ya, do it again!"

Now we were quickly becoming famous, and pride rushed into our hearts. All reasoning fled from our minds, and it was time to show off.

Humanity of the disciples

Jesus didn't pick saints to follow him. He picked young men with all the human failings that most young adults face. Any quick review of the lives of Jesus's disciples would show us that each one of them battled with the personality quirks, pride, and temptations that we also struggle with.

Nathanael

Let's take a look at Nathanael. While Nathanael was a noble-minded seeker of truth, he was also dogged with both pride and prejudice:

> *The day following Jesus would go forth into Galilee, and findeth Philip, and saith unto him, 'Follow me.' Now Philip was of Bethsaida, the city of Andrew and Peter. Philip findeth Nathanael, and saith unto him, 'We have found him, of whom Moses in the law, and the prophets, did write, Jesus of Nazareth, the son of Joseph.' And Nathanael said*

41

unto him, 'Can there any good thing come out of Nazareth?' Philip saith unto him, 'Come and see.'

Jesus saw Nathanael coming to him, and saith of him, 'behold an Israelite indeed, in whom is no guile!' Nathanael saith unto him, 'Whence knowest thou me?' Jesus answered and said unto him, 'Before that Philip called thee, when thou wast under the fig tree, I saw thee.' Nathanael answered and saith unto him, 'Rabbi, thou art the Son of God; thou art the King of Israel.'

Jesus answered and said unto him, 'because I said unto thee, I saw thee under the fig tree, believest thou? Thou shalt see greater things than these.' And he saith unto him, 'Verily, verily, I say unto you, hereafter ye shall see heaven open, and the angels of God ascending and descending upon the Son of man.' (John 1:43–51 KJV).

Nathanael or Bartholomew?

In the Gospels of Matthew, Mark, and Luke, the name Nathanael doesn't appear, but the name Bartholomew does. Matthew, Mark, and Luke tell of Bartholomew as being Philip's friend. Then in the Gospel of John, Nathanael is linked to Philip. From these references, we surmise that he was Nathanael Bartholomew or Nathanael, the son of Tolmai.

We have found the one

Philip and Nathanael were close friends. They were both from small towns in Galilee. Philip was from Bethsaida, and Nathanael was from Cana.

After Jesus called Philip to follow him, Philip immediately went and found his friend Nathanael and said, *"We have found him, of whom Moses in the law, and the prophets, did write, Jesus of Nazareth, the son of Joseph."*

Philip and Nathanael had probably frequently discussed the witness of Moses and the prophets concerning the coming of the Messiah, but what catches us off guard is Nathanael's response.

Are you kidding me? Nazareth?

"Nazareth! Can anything good come from there?" Nathanael asked.

Galileans despised people from Nazareth. Nathanael's pride and prejudice are displayed boldly here with this curt response. Not only did Nathanael view the town of Nazareth, just a few miles away, as insignificant, he also revealed a young man's pride in his village over the rival village.

In Nathanael's defense, as he and Philip studied the prophecies about the coming Messiah, they may have focused on the facts that He would be born in Bethlehem (see Micah 5:2; Matthew 2:1); that He would be a light to Galilee (see Isaiah 9:1–2; Matthew 4:13–16); and missed that He would come out of Egypt (see Hosea 11:1; Matthew 2:14–15); and that He would be called a Nazarene (see Isaiah 11:1; Matthew 2:23).

Philip was not fazed and didn't enter into an argument with Nathanael. He simply replied, *"Come and see."*

No guile

I think we find out why Jesus chose him when we look at the next verse. When Nathanael came to Jesus, our Lord saw him spiritually.

Jesus knew what was in his heart: *"behold an Israelite indeed, in whom is no guile!"*

Quite a compliment! A man without guile, without hypocrisy, having integrity, a true seeker of truth, without craftiness. He doesn't look for wrong motives but takes those he meets at face value.

But pride and prejudice

Nathanael, without deception—Jesus said so—was a man full of pride and prejudice! A man may have some virtues but lack others. He may not have been a hypocrite, but he may still have had hatred in his heart. He may have been a good person but still had the poison of prejudice. He may not have been crafty, but he was prideful and conceited. Nathanael had no guile, but that did not make him perfect. He still struggled with his pride. He thought himself better than these others, especially those from Nazareth.

What to do with prejudice and pride

But what do we do with prejudice and pride? *"'Come and see,' said Philip."*

Pride and prejudice are sneaky sins and are easily overlooked in a person's life. We are inherently selfish people, and as such, we look at most situations and other people through the prism of "How does this affect me?" "How does this make me feel?" Then our pride rises up and we feel justified to feel that way. When this happens, if we catch it, the remedy is: Come to Jesus Christ!

> *But he gives us more grace. That is why Scripture says: 'God opposes the proud but gives grace to the humble.' Submit yourselves, then, to God. Resist the devil, and he will flee from you. Come near to God and he will come near to you. Wash your hands, you sinners, and purify your hearts, you double-minded. Grieve, mourn and wail. Change your laughter to mourning and your joy to gloom. Humble yourselves before the Lord, and he will lift you up.* (James 4:4–6 NIV)

> *Finally, all of you, live in harmony with one another; be sympathetic, love as brothers, be compassionate and humble.* (1 Peter 3:8 NIV)

> *Be humble and gentle. Be patient with each other, making allowance for each other's faults because of your love. Try always to be led along together by the Holy Spirit and so be at peace with one another. We are all parts of one body, we have the same Spirit, and we have all been called to the same glorious future. For us there is only one Lord, one faith, one baptism, and we all have the same God and Father who is over us all and in us all, and living through every part of us. However, Christ has given each of us special abilities—whatever he wants us to have out of his rich storehouse of gifts.* (Ephesians 4:2–7 TLB)

In order to break the bondage of pride, I must humbly come to Jesus. Come and see Jesus.

I must humble myself before Jesus and submit to Him, making Him Lord of my life. I need to recognize my pride and my prejudice and resist the devil who wants to plant these in my heart.

I must repent of these sins, *"grieve, mourn and wail,"* as the scripture says, and ask for forgiveness.

Then I must work at living in harmony with others. I must be patient, sympathetic, compassionate, and humble. I must love others as myself.

These scriptures seem to place all the pressure on us and our work but don't miss, *"But he gives us more grace"* (James 4:4). He will give us grace, and He will draw near to us.

Come to Jesus!

He will remove your prejudice. He will show you that the God who has made of one blood all nations of men, has with the blood of One redeemed all who will come to Him.

Come and see Jesus!

Jesus knows us

Nathanael asked this Jesus whom he had never met a question. "I don't know you. How do you know me?"

Jesus answered, "Before Philip found you, I saw you under the fig tree."

Jesus saw him while he was sitting in his quiet place probably meditating, thinking of God. Praying silently. In Nathanael's quiet time with God, Jesus saw him. Jesus knew his innermost thoughts. Jesus knew the true Nathanael.

And He sees you too! As you come to Him, meditate on Him, pray to Him. He sees you and knows you. He knows your innermost thoughts. He knows your weaknesses and strengths. He loves you and calls you to believe in Him.

Will you come and see Him?

Nathanael quickly believed Jesus was the Messiah, the God of the universe, the king of Israel. Jesus was amazed. The conversation was hardly begun, and the man was so quick to believe. There had been so little evidence.

Then Jesus made him a promise. *"You believe because I told you I saw you under the fig tree. You shall see greater things than that. I tell you the truth, you shall see heaven open, and the angels of God ascending and descending on the Son of Man"* (John 1:50–51 NIV).

That day Nathanael followed Jesus. That day Jesus began the work of grace in Nathanael's life. That day Jesus began the process of healing Nathanael of his pride and prejudice.

Back at The Clam

Off I jumped again. Down I went. Not thinking about the swell. Not thinking about the depth of the water. Not thinking about breaking off the dive quickly.

Not thinking!

My swan dive was once again near perfect. I straightened my arms, locked my elbows, and clenched my fists just before impact, and down I went. I broke my dive too deep and *bam!*

"Scrape!"

I had hit a rock. I came to the surface dazed and confused. What I thought was saltwater dripping down my face was oddly red in color. My head hurt. My face hurt. My chest hurt. Fortunately for me, I had only grazed the rock. I felt my head then looked at my hand.

Yep, I'm bleeding but keep your head, Brian, I thought.

"Hey, Daniel!" I shouted, keeping in character. "I think I hit my head on a blummin' rock!"

"That's smashing!" came his reply.

I wish I could say I learned my lesson about showing off but all I understood at that time was a great day had come to an abrupt, bloody, and painful end.

CHAPTER 5

THE SUBMISSION OF A MAN
"MEN WHO FOLLOW"

I earned the privilege of driving in my sophomore year of high school. I passed driver's training in school and received my permit. It was now time to learn how to drive a car with a manual transmission. (A stick shift, for those of you younger than me.)

My brother-in-law, Ed, took me to the San Diego Stadium driving my 1964 Ford Falcon, with the *three-on-the-tree* transmission to teach me how to drive a stick shift. We jerked and bounced across the giant parking lot of the stadium; it's a wonder neither of us sustained whiplash.

Finally, I received my driver's license; I could drive the stick fairly well. Except for starting out on an uphill street, but I wasn't worried about that—yet.

I knew I had arrived at adulthood! Sixteen years old, could drive, had my own car, and knew everything. So, of course, that meant that I would inform my parents of what I was going to do and where I was going. Or just do it and tell them later. Needless to say, this led to some battles with my parents; I had forgotten who was still in control.

One stormy Wednesday night, I decided I would drive to a youth group meeting at the El Cajon Foursquare Church some twenty miles away instead of going to my youth group at the San

Diego Foursquare Church, which was much closer. Why, you ask? I'm a sixteen-year-old boy! Still confused?

Okay, a beautiful blonde girl, who attended the other youth group, had gotten my attention at summer camp, and she invited me to her youth group meeting.

As I headed out the door, my dad asked where I was going on this unusually rainy Wednesday evening, and I told him. He gently responded that he didn't think that was a good idea.

"Okay, bye," I replied on my way out the door.

Why do men in particular struggle to follow Jesus? I think there are two main reasons—pride and submission. We already looked at pride in the last chapter; now let's explore the topic of submission.

The rich ruler

In the Gospels of Matthew, Mark, and Luke, there is a story of a rich ruler coming to Jesus with the question of what he had to do to be saved:

And a certain ruler asked him, saying, 'Good Master, what shall I do to inherit eternal life?' And Jesus said unto him, 'Why callest thou me good? none is good, save one, that is, God. Thou knowest the commandments, do not commit adultery, do not kill, do not steal, do not bear false witness, Honor thy father and thy mother.' And he said, 'All these have I kept from my youth up.'

Now when Jesus heard these things, he said unto him, 'yet lackest thou one thing: sell all that thou hast, and distribute unto the poor, and thou shalt have treasure in heaven: and come, follow me.' And when he heard this, he was very sorrowful: for he was very rich. And when Jesus saw that he was very sorrowful, he said, 'how hardly shall they that have riches enter into the kingdom of God! For it is

easier for a camel to go through a needle's eye, than
for a rich man to enter into the kingdom of God.'
   And they that heard it said, 'Who then can be
saved?' And he said, 'The things which are impossi-
ble with men are possible with God.' (Luke 18:18–
27 KJV)

This rich ruler came to Jesus seeking the assurance of eternal life. Jesus told him to follow the commandments. There are Ten Commandments. Six of the ten deal with interpersonal relationships. Jesus listed five of these. I find it interesting that Jesus would remind this man of five out of the six. Did He purposefully leave out, "You shall not covet anything that belongs to your neighbor?"

I don't think Jesus did or said anything unintentionally, so why leave this one out? I don't know. But I can suggest some possibilities. Maybe because this man was a ruler and was wealthy, he didn't have a problem with covetousness. This reason doesn't hold much weight when compared to the story of King David. (David was a rich ruler as well, but he coveted Bathsheba, the wife of Uriah the Hittite.) A more likely answer is that this would be one of the commandments that this man struggled with. Possibly causing him to be convicted of this sin, make him think about doing another good deed, and miss Jesus's real point that salvation does not come from good deeds.

Jesus was not about to point out another good deed for the ruler to accomplish; instead, He showed him that he needed to humble himself and submit to Jesus as Lord of his life.

Submission in service

First, Jesus said, "*You still lack one thing. Sell everything you have and give to the poor...* " (verse 22a).

Kingdom living is very different from the way the world lives; it's the opposite.

This man was a ruler; he was used to being served. If he asked for something to be done, it was done and by someone else. He was in charge, and people served him. By Jesus telling him to sell everything and give it all to the poor, he was being instructed to stop being in charge and start serving others. He was being told to humble himself and submit to others. He was being taught the difference between self-love and servanthood. Self-love serves the self while servanthood serves others. Jesus taught this kingdom principle many times.

Matthew 19:30 (NIV) says, *"But many who are first will be last, and many who are last will be first."*

Treasure in heaven

Secondly, Jesus said, *"And you will have treasure in heaven."*

The Bible says this ruler had *"great wealth."* This guy was rich! Much of the time, the accumulation of money has been presented as a sign of God's blessing. Maybe this was part of this guy's problem? He felt like God has blessed him with riches, so he was going to bless God by following the Ten Commandments.

He still felt empty, prompting his question of Jesus. What could he do to get eternal life? How much would it cost him to acquire life everlasting? Jesus was teaching him the kingdom principle that treasure on earth is not the same as treasure in heaven. Treasure on earth has to do with the law, works, and the accumulation of goods while treasure in heaven has to do with service, submission, obedience, and grace.

Be a follower

Finally, Jesus said, *"Then come, follow me."* Jesus was asking him to submit to Christ as his new ruler and follow Him. Jesus was teaching him the kingdom principle that the rulers here on earth will become the followers in heaven, and the submitted followers, the servants of all on earth, will become the leaders and rulers in heaven.

"Sitting down, Jesus called the Twelve and said, 'If anyone wants to be first, he must be the very last, and the servant of all'" (Mark 9:35 NIV).

Submission of Jesus

Jesus not only taught about the importance of submission and servanthood, He also lived it. Let's take a look at some of the examples from scripture:

> *In the beginning was the Word, and the Word was with God, and the Word was God. He was with God in the beginning. Through him all things were made; without him, nothing was made that has been made.* (John 1:1–3 NIV)

> *The Word became flesh and made his dwelling among us. We have seen his glory, the glory of the One and Only, who came from the Father, full of grace and truth.* (John 1:14 NIV)

Jesus was and is the eternal God, but He submitted to the Father and humbly took on a human body so He could dwell among us to show us the way back to the Father.

Jesus was the Creator of the universe. All things were made by Him, but He voluntarily submitted Himself to human frailty, experiencing temptation,[1] hunger,[2] tiredness,[3] grief,[4] and pain.[5]

Jesus was and is the King of kings and Lord of lords[6] yet He humbled Himself to serve us and be the sacrifice for our sins.[7]

Jesus, the omniscient God, told us that He did nothing by Himself but submitted to the Father by only doing what He first saw His Father doing.[8]

---

[1] Matthew 4:1.
[2] Matthew 4:2.
[3] Luke 8:23.
[4] Luke 19:41, John 11:35.
[5] Mark 15:16–20; John 19:1–5.
[6] Timothy 6:15, Revelation 17:14, Revelation 19:16.
[7] Mark 10:45.
[8] John 5:19.

Finally, as we have seen, Jesus was fully God and fully man at the same time while He was here on earth. As a man, He modeled for us what submission is and how to be a submitted person. In the garden of Gethsemane, on the Mount of Olives, Jesus, too, struggled with submission. He asked His Father if there was some other way His plan could be accomplished. He prayed so hard about this that He actually sweat blood, finally concluding with *"yet not my will, but yours be done."* He showed us that at times, submission is difficult but vital:

> *Jesus went out as usual to the Mount of Olives, and his disciples followed him. On reaching the place, he said to them, 'Pray that you will not fall into temptation.' He withdrew about a stone's throw beyond them, knelt down, and prayed, 'Father, if you are willing, take this cup from me; yet not my will, but yours be done.' An angel from heaven appeared to him and strengthened him. And being in anguish, he prayed more earnestly, and his sweat was like drops of blood falling to the ground. (Luke 22:39–4 NIV)*

The struggle of submission

I believe men struggle with submission because of how God made them. He made them to be a covering over the women and children, to work hard, and to be the provider for his family. After the fall in the garden of Eden, Adam was commanded to work and provide for his family.[9]

The Bible says that wives are to submit to their husbands,[10] and children are to obey their parents.[11] Because of this, I think men find it hard to submit to others and even to the Lord.

---

[9] Genesis 3:17–19.
[10] Ephesians 5:22.
[11] Ephesians 6:1.

Another possibility is, either by improper teaching, society through the ages, or just unwillingness on man's part to *"rightly divide the word of truth,"*[12] men sometimes live as though they are the rulers of all things.

When the scriptures are taken in context, the Word of God is always in balance. Quite often the topic of submission is out of balance. Authoritarians wield their favorite submission scriptures like a sword to accomplish their goals. Scriptures like *"Everyone must submit himself to the governing authorities,"*[13] and *"Wives submit to your husbands"*[14] are used as a method of control over others. But the whole of the Bible on this topic is balanced; with multiple verses, the scripture teaches mutual submission.[15]

The focus of Ephesians on mutual submission

Let's take a look at Ephesians 5:21–6:1 (KJV) in context:

> *Submitting yourselves one to another in the fear of God. Wives, submit yourselves unto your own husbands, as unto the Lord. For the husband is the head of the wife, even as Christ is the head of the church: and he is the savior of the body. Therefore as the church is subject unto Christ, so let the wives be to their own husbands in everything. Husbands, love your wives, even as Christ also loved the church, and gave himself for it; That he might sanctify and cleanse it with the washing of water by the word, That he might present it to himself a glorious church, not having spot, or wrinkle, or any such thing; but that it should be holy and without blemish.*

---

[12] 2 Timothy 2:15.
[13] Romans 13:1, 5.
[14] Ephesians 5:22.
[15] 1 Corinthians 16:16; Ephesians 5:21–28; Hebrews 12:9, 13:17; James 4:7; 1 Peter 2:13.

> *So ought men to love their wives as their own bodies. He that loveth his wife loveth himself. For no man ever yet hated his own flesh; but nourisheth and cherisheth it, even as the Lord the church: For we are members of his body, of his flesh, and of his bones.*
>
> *For this cause shall a man leave his father and mother, and shall be joined unto his wife, and they two shall be one flesh. This is a great mystery: but I speak concerning Christ and the church. Nevertheless let every one of you in particular so love his wife even as himself; and the wife see that she reverence her husband. Children, obey your parents in the Lord: for this is right.*

Remember, when this portion of scripture was written by Paul, he was writing a letter to be read by this church congregation and passed along to other bodies of believers. There were no chapter headings, chapters, or verse numbers. Reading and studying it in context means the whole letter fits perfectly together, and though there are different subjects, they all flow from the writer's one purpose. Paul's intent was to unveil the *mystery* of the church. Paul points out that God's intention was to form a body, called the church, to express Jesus's fullness on earth. That body must be united as one people—both Jew and Gentile—among whom God himself could dwell. Paul wanted the church to be mature and empowered to overcome the evil in the world.

To this end, Paul spoke of mutual submission (verse 21), wives submitting to their husbands (verses 22–23), husbands submitting to Christ (verses 23–24), and children submitting to their parents (chapter 6 verse 1).

Particularly to men, Paul emphasizes that man is to submit to Christ as head of the church. The man is to love, honor, and respect his wife as much as Christ loved the church. He points out that Jesus died for the church because of His love for the body of believers, so the husband must love his wife in the same manner, willing to live for her, die for her, and love her as he loves himself.

A mature Christian man does this; he then earns, not demands, love, respect, and submission from his wife. Just as Christ has earned the love, respect, and submission of man.

When a Christian marriage and family are following and obeying the scriptures, they portray a picture of what the Christian church is to be to the world. When a Christian church is following and obeying the scriptures, it portrays Christ's body and intention for the salvation of the world.

Maturity begins

I actually remember what the topic of the Bible study over in El Cajon was that evening. It was about submission: *"Children, obey your parents in the Lord, for this is right"* (Ephesians 6:1).

On the way home, it was raining hard. I was keeping up with the flow of traffic, but a highway patrol officer pulled me over. He said I was going too fast for the conditions of the road. I don't remember that from driver's education.

I got my first speeding ticket.

Now this may seem trivial in life's scheme of events, but the Holy Spirit used it to convict me of my sin of rebellion and lack of submission. My life began to change in this area that very night.

I began to ask permission again and tried to obey. My dad, who was a very wise man, noticed. Soon when I would ask his permission to go someplace or do something, he began to ask me what I thought about my request, if I thought it was a good idea or a wise decision. This opened huge communication doors with my father and with Jesus. I began to mature as a person and as a young Christian man.

Learning to submit will do that. It teaches us humility. It teaches us how to serve. It teaches us how to know Jesus, not only as Savior but as the Lord of our lives.

CHAPTER 6

THE JOY OF A MAN
"IT'S PARTY TIME!"

In 1991, I remember watching the movie *Father of the Bride* and laughing uncontrollably. George Banks, played by Steve Martin, is the father of the bride. It's a story about his emotions while helping to plan his daughter's wedding. It's hilarious and moving as he navigates through the planning and ultimately gives away his daughter in marriage. The things he does and says during this period are sidesplitting as he jumps from one emotion to another. At times he appears to have lost his senses, while other scenes show him as the understanding, sensitive, and wise father.

I love comedies; Steve Martin has always been one of my favorite actors. I was thoroughly entertained by the movie, but it held no additional meaning for me as my daughter, Brianna, was only ten years old at the time.

Then fifteen years later, it was my turn to be the father of the bride. I became George Banks.

I remember telling people how much per plate it was costing me and how many people were coming. I remember sitting with Brianna planning the big day and she, like Annie Banks, was worried about how much it would cost her dad. Scenes from the movie would flash through my head after one of my odd actions would mirror George. During this time, it's almost frightening how many different emotions can be experienced simultaneously; it's like a witch's brew churning inside. Worry, concern, and fear are all mixed up with pride, excitement, and happiness. Eventually, joy overrides all of them.

Emotional people

God created all people with emotions to help them navigate through the seasons of their life and men are no exception. So then why is it common for men to struggle with expressing their emotions? For many, it's what was patterned for them by other men in their early stages of growth. For others, it's what they had been taught. For most, it's the feeling that they need to be in control of their emotions.

Men are taught to be strong, in control, and reserved; "real men don't cry." Why does it seem that a man can be joyful and vocal about his favorite sports team winning, but when it comes to expressing a joyful relationship with Jesus, he becomes very timid?

Are we really controlling our emotions, or are our emotions actually controlling us?

God wants us to express our emotions, especially when it comes to our relationship with Him.

God is a joyful God!

Jesus loved to party!

Men should be joyful men!

Whom should we invite?

I remember sitting with my daughter to decide whom we should invite to the wedding. The main questions were: "Whom do we want to celebrate this joyous occasion with?" "Who are the most important people in all our lives?" "All of the family?" (I come from a big family; my mom is one of ten kids). "Even my wife Robann's side of the family too?" "Which friends and colleagues should we like to invite?" The list got really big really fast, and like George, I kept wanting to cull the invitations.

In the Gospel of John, we have a story about the wedding in Cana where Jesus performed His first miracle:

> On the third day a wedding took place at Cana in Galilee. Jesus' mother was there, and Jesus and his disciples had also been invited to the wedding. When the wine was gone, Jesus' mother said to him, 'They have no more wine.' 'Dear woman, why do you involve me?' Jesus replied. 'My time has not yet come.' His mother said to the servants, 'do whatever he tells you.' Nearby stood six stone water jars, the kind used by the Jews for ceremonial washing, each holding from twenty to thirty gallons. Jesus said to the servants, 'Fill the jars with water'; so, they filled them to the brim. Then he told them, 'now draw some out and take it to the master of the banquet.' They did so, and the master of the banquet tasted the water that had been turned into wine. He did not realize where it had come from, though the servants who had drawn the water knew. Then he called the bridegroom aside and said, 'everyone brings out the choice wine first and then the cheaper wine after the guests have had too much to drink, but you have saved the best till now.' This, the first of his miraculous signs, Jesus performed at Cana in Galilee. He thus revealed his glory, and his disciples put their faith in him. (John 2:1–11 NIV)

Verse 2 says, *"Jesus and his disciples had also been invited to the wedding."*

When this young couple sat down to ask the question "Whom should we invite to our wedding?", they decided that Jesus and His disciple should come.

Besides family, who were the important people in this couple's lives?

Jesus and His disciples!

They were all friends. Jesus didn't crash this party; He was invited. Mary didn't invite Him; the bride and groom did.

This was a joyous occasion. This was a celebration that the couple wanted Jesus and His disciples to enjoy with them because they were friends, and they knew Jesus loved to party!

As the story goes, a need arose, and Jesus turned water into wine. Because Jesus was part of their lives, when a need arose, Jesus the guest became Jesus the host and supplied their need.

This is true for us as well. Jesus wants to have a joyous relationship with us. He wants to be our friend. If we will invite Him into our lives, to be a guest in our soul, He will become the host supplying all our needs and filling our lives with joy.

Time to party!

In the fifteenth chapter of the Gospel of Luke, Jesus tells three parables: the parable of the lost sheep, the parable of the lost coin, and the parable of the prodigal son.

In these parables, we see that Jesus loves to party and what He likes to celebrate:

> *What man of you, having an hundred sheep, if he lose one of them, doth not leave the ninety and nine in the wilderness, and go after that which is lost, until he find it? And when he hath found it, he layeth it on his shoulders, rejoicing. And when he cometh home, he calleth together his friends and neighbours, saying unto them, rejoice with me; for I have found my sheep which was lost. I say unto you, that likewise joy shall be in heaven over one sinner that repenteth, more than over ninety and nine just persons, which need no repentance. (Luke 15:4–7 KJV)*

Notice what Jesus says the shepherd does when he finds his one lost sheep. He throws a party. He calls his friends and neighbors to come and rejoice with him at his *sheep-finding party*. Why does he do this? Why is he joyful? Because that which was lost is now found.

Here, Jesus tells us that all of heaven throws a party each time one sinner repents of his sin. Heaven rejoices every time someone receives Jesus as Savior because he who was lost is now found.

> *Either what woman having ten pieces of silver,*
> *if she lose one piece, doth not light a candle, and*
> *sweep the house, and seek diligently till she find it?*
> *And when she hath found it, she calleth her friends*
> *and her neighbours together, saying, rejoice with*
> *me; for I have found the piece which I had lost.*
> *Likewise, I say unto you, there is joy in the presence*
> *of the angels of God over one sinner that repenteth.*
> (Luke 15:8–10 KJV)

Notice what Jesus says the woman does when she finds her one lost coin. She throws a party. She calls her friends and neighbors to come and rejoice with her at her *coin-finding party*. Why does she do this? Why is she joyful? Because that which was lost is now found. Here, Jesus tells us that the angels throw a party each time one sinner repents of his sin. The angels of God rejoice every time someone receives Jesus as Savior because he who was lost is now found.

> *And he said, 'a certain man had two sons: And*
> *the younger of them said to his father,' 'father, give*
> *me the portion of goods that falleth to me.' And he*
> *divided unto them his living. And not many days*
> *after the younger son gathered all together, and took*
> *his journey into a far country, and there wasted his*
> *substance with riotous living. And when he had*
> *spent all, there arose a mighty famine in that land;*
> *and he began to be in want. And he went and joined*
> *himself to a citizen of that country; and he sent him*
> *into his fields to feed swine. And he would fain have*

filled his belly with the husks that the swine did eat: and no man gave unto him.

And when he came to himself, he said, 'how many hired servants of my father have bread enough and to spare, and I perish with hunger! I will arise and go to my father, and will say unto him, father, I have sinned against heaven, and before thee, and am no more worthy to be called thy son: make me as one of thy hired servants.'

And he arose, and came to his father. But when he was yet a great way off, his father saw him, and had compassion, and ran, and fell on his neck, and kissed him. And the son said unto him, 'father, I have sinned against heaven, and in thy sight, and am no more worthy to be called thy son.' But the father said to his servants, 'bring forth the best robe, and put it on him; and put a ring on his hand, and shoes on his feet: And bring hither the fatted calf, and kill it; and let us eat, and be merry: For this my son was dead, and is alive again; he was lost, and is found.' And they began to be merry.

"Now his elder son was in the field: and as he came and drew nigh to the house, he heard music and dancing. And he called one of the servants, and asked what these things meant. And he said unto him, 'Thy brother is come; and thy father hath killed the fatted calf, because he hath received him safe and sound.'

And he was angry, and would not go in: therefore came his father out, and intreated him. And he answering said to his father, 'Lo, these many years do I serve thee, neither transgressed I at any time thy commandment: and yet thou never gavest me a kid, that I might make merry with my friends:

But as soon as this thy son was come, which hath devoured thy living with harlots, thou hast killed for him the fatted calf.' And he said unto him, 'Son, thou art ever with me, and all that I have is thine. It was meet that we should make merry, and be glad: for this thy brother was dead, and is alive again; and was lost, and is found.' (Luke 15:11–32 KJV)

After squandering all of his wealth, the prodigal son finally *"came to his senses"* and went home. We don't know how long this son was gone, but it was long enough for him to use up his entire inheritance and for a famine to ravage the land.

Verse 20 tells us, *"But while he was still a long way off, his father saw him and was filled with compassion for him; he ran to his son, threw his arms around him, and kissed him."*

Had the father gone daily to the front gate and looked a long way off in the distance to see if today might be the day his son comes home? Waiting, hoping, yearning for his son to come home? I like to think so.

Again, notice what Jesus says the father does when his son finally comes back home. He throws a party. He calls his servants to come and rejoice with him at his *son's homecoming party*. Why does he do this? Why is he joyful? Because he who was lost is now found. He told his older son why he was throwing the party: *"But we had to celebrate and be glad, because this brother of yours was dead and is alive again; he was lost and is found."*

Did all heaven throw a party too? Did the angels pass out party hats and those blowout party whistles? You betcha! This is what happens each time one sinner repents of his sin. Heaven rejoices every time someone receives Jesus as Savior because he who was dead is now alive again!

Jesus loves these kinds of parties!

The final party

Have I said that Jesus loves to party? One more story confirms this. In Revelation 19:6–9, we're told of the final party of this age. It's called the marriage supper of the Lamb:

> And I heard as it were the voice of a great multitude, and as the voice of many waters, and as the voice of mighty thunderings, saying, 'alleluia: for the Lord God omnipotent reigneth. Let us be glad and rejoice, and give honour to him: For the marriage of the Lamb is come, and his wife hath made herself ready. And to her was granted that she should be arrayed in fine linen, clean and white: for the fine linen is the righteousness of saints.'
> And he saith unto me, 'Write, blessed are they which are called unto the marriage supper of the Lamb.' And he saith unto me, 'these are the true sayings of God.'

One of the first things Jesus will do, for all of us who have received Him as Lord and Savior, when we get to heaven is throw us a party. We will be glad and rejoice. We will shout "Hallelujah!" We will be given new clothes and then we will feast with Jesus!

Joy versus happiness

There is a difference between biblical joy and happiness. Happiness is temporal. It is experienced circumstantially. It is a response to circumstances in our lives that bring a feeling of happiness. There is nothing wrong with feeling happy or having an emotional response of happiness when something good happens in our lives, but it is physical gladness, not necessarily spiritual contentment. This is outward cheerfulness, not inward joy.

Biblical joy is deeper than happiness. It is a party in the soul. This joy can be felt even when facing circumstances that are trying or terrible. Philippians explains that joy is a calmness in the soul, a peace that defies understanding.[1] Biblical joy only comes from Jesus and is appropriated by faith in Him, filling us with an *"inexpressible and glorious joy."*[2] Jesus's joy can actually give us spiritual and even physical strength.[3] It is also part of the fruit of the Spirit that comes with salvation from the Holy Spirit.[4]

Biblical joy is nurtured by God's word and by our relationship with the Father, the Son, and the Holy Spirit. If we stay connected to Jesus like a healthy grape branch stays connected to the vine, we will become obedient Christians in action, falling more and more in love with Jesus as His love fills us.

If we abide in Jesus, He will fill us with His joy, and our joy will be complete. As we continue to remain in Christ, we will bear fruit. This fruit shows that we are Jesus's disciples as we mature in Him. We will want to share this life with others and see those who were lost be found through salvation in Jesus. This kind of fruit is everlasting. It will bring us joy so that we will want to throw a party too.[5]

Joyful men

When Jesus was arrested, all of His disciples, except John, ran for their lives in fear. Peter even denied knowing Jesus. After Jesus's resurrection, ascension to heaven, and the Holy Spirit's filling of the apostles on the day of Pentecost, these men became altogether different people.

Once timid, fearful, and unsure of themselves, they were transformed into world changers. They became bold preachers of the gospel of Christ, seeing many people turn from their sinful ways and receive Jesus as their Lord and Savior. Did they still struggle with emotions? I'm sure they did. But now, through the power of the Holy

---

[1] Philippians 4:7.
[2] 1 Peter 1:8.
[3] Nehemiah 8:10.
[4] Galatians 5:16–26.
[5] John 15:1–17.

Spirit, they fulfilled Jesus's command to *"go into all the world and preach the Gospel."*[6]

Most of them were martyred for their vocal faith in Jesus. Remember the story of Stephen?[7]

> *When they heard these things, they were cut to the heart, and they gnashed on him with their teeth. But he, being full of the Holy Ghost, looked up stedfastly into heaven, and saw the glory of God, and Jesus standing on the right hand of God, and said, 'Behold, I see the heavens opened, and the Son of man standing on the right hand of God.'*
>
> *Then they cried out with a loud voice, and stopped their ears, and ran upon him with one accord, and cast him out of the city, and stoned him: and the witnesses laid down their clothes at a young man's feet, whose name was Saul.*
>
> *And they stoned Stephen, calling upon God, and saying, 'Lord Jesus, receive my spirit.' And he kneeled down, and cried with a loud voice, 'Lord, lay not this sin to their charge.' And when he had said this, he fell asleep.* (Acts 7:54–60 KJV)

They showed us what real men are made of.

They showed us that real men are joyful men!

Men who have been born again and have a relationship with Jesus will love to party, just like Jesus did!

---

6   Mark 16:15.
7   Acts 6:8–7:60.

CHAPTER 7

THE GIFTS OF A MAN

Pat was a multigifted person. He was friendly, outgoing, and sure of himself. He was funny and a super athlete. He was good-looking and tall (well, everyone seems tall to me). Pat was my cousin and my idol. In fact, all of the cousins looked up to Pat, our elder statesman, our confidant, our comedian, and our celebrity.

When we all played football together, which was often, everybody wanted to be on Pat's team; he always won. When we were in a crowd, everyone flocked around Pat. When we met girls at the beach, ya, you get the idea.

This didn't seem to bother me much; at least I was hanging out with Pat and that made me important. I was insecure and shy, so being with Pat made me somebody of value.

When I think about the apostle Andrew, I wonder if he was somewhat like this when it came to his relationship with his older brother, Peter.

First to follow Jesus

> *Again the next day after John stood, and two of his disciples; And looking upon Jesus as he walked, he saith, 'Behold the Lamb of God!' And the two disciples heard him speak, and they followed Jesus.*

Then Jesus turned, and saw them following, and saith unto them, 'What seek ye? They said unto him, Rabbi, (which is to say, being interpreted, Master,) where dwellest thou?' He saith unto them, 'Come and see.' They came and saw where he dwelt, and abode with him that day: for it was about the tenth hour. One of the two which heard John speak, and followed him, was Andrew, Simon Peter's brother. He first findeth his own brother Simon, and saith unto him, 'We have found the Messias,' which is, being interpreted, the Christ. And he brought him to Jesus. And when Jesus beheld him, he said, 'Thou art Simon the son of Jona: thou shalt be called Cephas,' which is by interpretation, A stone. (John 1:35–42 KJV)

We first get to meet Andrew in the Gospel of John. He and John, the beloved author of the Gospel, were following John the Baptist. It tells us that they were two of John's disciples. Eagerly they listened to the Baptist's teaching about the coming Messiah, following him wherever he went. Then one day, John stopped, pointed to someone passing by, and said, *"Look, the Lamb of God!"*

Immediately, these two enthusiastic young men turned around and began following Jesus. When Jesus saw them following Him, He stopped and asked them what they wanted. I wonder if it startled them, cause saying as they did, *"Teacher, where are you staying?"* doesn't seem to me like an appropriate response. At any rate, Jesus invited them to come and see. They both spent the day with Jesus. It was so life changing for them that John recorded the very hour it happened.

It's interesting that John, the writer of the Gospel, never refers to himself in the first person. Here he is *"one of the two"* disciples. He also gives a qualifier for the other disciple, Andrew. He doesn't say, "My friend, Andrew, and I." He doesn't just say, "Andrew." He says, *"Andrew, Simon Peter's brother."* It's as if he knows people will ask, "Andrew who?"

Now Andrew and John are super important people. They are the first to find and follow the long-awaited Messiah. Andrew could have kept this to himself and maybe he could have become someone other than "Andrew who?" He doesn't though; his initial action is to go tell his brother Simon and bring him to Jesus.

Wouldn't you know it? The first thing Jesus does is compliment Simon and change his name to Peter the Rock.

Andrew immediately went back to second place, back to looking up to his older sibling, back to, you know, *Simon Peter's brother*.

Andrew and John were the first to follow Jesus, yet they are never mentioned first in any list of the twelve disciples. Peter is always mentioned first, and Andrew is second and even fourth in the Gospel of Mark and the book of Acts.

Always second string

I think Peter was like my cousin Pat. He was the star quarterback at Jerusalem High School. He knew all the girls on the shore of Galilee. He was a successful businessman (owning his own fishing business). He was also a big talker and probably the funny man among the disciples.

I like to think that there was mutual respect among these brothers. Andrew came to him with this wild claim that he had met the long-awaited king of Israel, the One the prophets had spoken of often. There are many responses Peter could have given to his baby brother that we could easily imagine this boisterous leader of men giving, but he doesn't. Instead, he goes with Andrew to meet Jesus. What was it about Andrew's life that caused this quick response?

He brought a little boy

The next time John mentions Andrew is a few months later:

> *After these things Jesus went over the sea of Galilee, which is the sea of Tiberias. And a great multitude followed him, because they saw his mir-*

acles which he did on them that were diseased. And Jesus went up into a mountain, and there he sat with his disciples. And the passover, a feast of the Jews, was nigh. When Jesus then lifted up his eyes, and saw a great company come unto him, he saith unto Philip, 'Whence shall we buy bread, that these may eat?' And this he said to prove him: for he himself knew what he would do. Philip answered him, 'Two hundred pennyworth of bread is not sufficient for them, that every one of them may take a little.' (John 6:1–7 KJV)

I like to put myself in the middle of the stories I read in the Bible. I like to imagine that I'm there, seeing what Jesus was doing, thinking what the apostles might have thought, and feeling what the people could have felt.

When we come to this story from a chronological perspective, Jesus had just finished about an eight-month teaching tour, the disciples had just returned from their preaching mission, and they had all recently learned of the beheading of John the Baptist. Mark tells us, *"Then, because so many people were coming and going that they did not even have a chance to eat, he said to them, 'Come with me by yourselves to a quiet place and get some rest.' So, they went away by themselves in a boat to a solitary place"* (Mark 6:31–32a NIV).

They were all going through a mixed bag of emotions. They were exhausted, excited, eager to reunite and tell their stories, but also shocked, confused, and sad at the news of John. They all needed a vacation. So Jesus suggested going to Hawaii and resting. (Sorry, my imagination got away from me.) He invited them to a *quiet place* to rest.

But a large crowd from all over followed them. We're told it was at least five thousand men; we're not told how many women and children there were. Again, Mark tells us:

But many who saw them leaving recognized them and ran on foot from all the towns and got there ahead of them. When Jesus landed and saw a large crowd, he had compassion on them, because they were like sheep without a shepherd. So, he began teaching them many things. (Mark 6:32b–34 NIV)

After a long afternoon of sitting in the sun listening to Jesus teach, it was getting late. When the people followed Jesus earlier that day, they were not thinking of bringing fold-up chairs, blankets, water, or picnic lunches. They were too thrilled to see Jesus and were maybe anticipating seeing more miracles.

It was dinnertime, it was time to go home, people were tired, and the kids were cranky.

"By this time, it was late in the day, so his disciples came to him. 'This is a remote place,' they said, 'and it's already very late. Send the people away so they can go to the surrounding countryside and villages and buy themselves something to eat.' But he answered, 'You give them something to eat'" (Mark 6:35–37 NIV).

Indulge my imagination again, if you will. Phillip walks up to Jesus and says, "Hey, Jesus, it's getting pretty late, these people are tired and hungry, and by the way, so am I."

Jesus replies, "Yes, you're right. Why don't you go buy them all something to eat?"

Phillip stands there for the longest time, dumbfounded, and finally speaks up, "Are you kidding me?"

Silence, more silence. Finally, still not sure if Jesus is serious, he says, "I don't have any money!"

Andrew has been standing there this whole time listening to their discussion, so he enthusiastically offers help. "Guess what? I know of a boy here who has his picnic lunch with him. His mom packed him a lunch of five loaves of bread and two fish!"

Silence, more silence, awkward silence...

"Oh, but I guess that won't go too far."

One of his disciples, Andrew, Simon Peter's brother, saith unto him, 'There is a lad here, which

71

hath five barley loaves, and two small fishes: but what are they among so many?' And Jesus said, 'Make the men sit down.' Now there was much grass in the place. So the men sat down, in number about five thousand. And Jesus took the loaves; and when he had given thanks, he distributed to the disciples, and the disciples to them that were set down; and likewise of the fishes as much as they would. When they were filled, he said unto his disciples, 'Gather up the fragments that remain, that nothing be lost.' Therefore they gathered them together, and filled twelve baskets with the fragments of the five barley loaves, which remained over and above unto them that had eaten. (John 6:8–13 KJV)

Andrew? Andrew who? Oh, Simon Peter's brother! For the second time, John thinks we need clarification about who Andrew is.

Who is Andrew besides being Simon Peter's baby brother? He's a friendly person, a helpful person, and a man with a special gift.

Among thousands of people, Andrew befriended a young boy. He knew enough about this boy to know that his mom had packed him a picnic lunch and even its contents. Did the boy offer to share it with the apostle? Did Andrew tell the boy all about Jesus? About the fishing business? About his brother, Simon Peter? We don't know, but one thing is for sure—Andrew had the gift of evangelism. He knew how to bring people to Jesus.

We've seen him twice now, and he's always doing the same thing. He brought himself to Jesus, then he brought his brother Peter to Jesus, and now he's bringing a young boy to Jesus.

He brought the Greeks

And there were certain Greeks among them that came up to worship at the feast: The same came therefore to Philip, which was of Bethsaida of Galilee, and desired him, saying, 'Sir, we would see

Jesus.' Philip cometh and telleth Andrew: and again Andrew and Philip tell Jesus. And Jesus answered them, saying, 'The hour is come, that the Son of man should be glorified.' (John 12:20–23 KJV)

Here, one last time, we meet Andrew. It happens during the final week of Jesus's life on Palm Sunday. Jesus had just entered the city of Jerusalem riding on a donkey, as people waved palm branches and shouted, *"Hosanna! Blessed is he who comes in the name of the Lord! Blessed is the King of Israel!"*

Some Greeks had come to Jerusalem to worship at the Passover feast. Having heard about Jesus and now seeing Him, they want to meet Him. They came to Philip with the request, *"We would like to see Jesus."*

It seems strange that Philip didn't know what to do. Maybe it was because they were Greeks and therefore Gentiles. Maybe it was because Philip was still under the impression that Jesus had only come for the Jews. Confused about what to do, he came to ask Andrew. I think, because of Andrew's nature and what we have seen of him thus far, that there was no hesitation in his response. I believe Andrew told Philip something like, "Well, if they want to meet Jesus, then let's take them to Jesus!"

Did Andrew go and talk with them? Did he then bring them to Jesus and introduce them? We don't know, but I like to think it happened that way.

Always bringing others to Jesus

Andrew is mentioned only three times in the Gospels, but he is always doing the same thing: bringing people to Jesus. Andrew is a friendly disciple who always introduces others to Jesus.

Andrews don't have lots of gifts; they have just one gift, but their gift is the most important one of all:

And then he told them, 'You are to go into all the world and preach the Good News to everyone, everywhere. Those who believe and are baptized will be saved. But those who refuse to believe will be condemned.' (Mark 16:15–16 TLB)

Godly men are growing a tree that bears life-giving fruit, and all who win souls are wise. (Proverbs 11:30 TLB)

Only one gift?

My cousin Pat is multigifted. He seems to succeed in everything he does, and there is nothing he can't do. Peter was multigifted. He wrote two Epistles. He preached a great sermon on the day of Pentecost (in Acts chapter 2) where three thousand people were saved in one message. He worked miracles and was famous.

Andrew, on the other hand, had only one gift. Yet God used Andrew's one gift for the kingdom just as much as Peter's many gifts.

First Corinthians 3:6–8 (ASV) tells us, *"I planted, Apollos watered; but God gave the increase. So then neither is he that planteth anything, neither he that watereth; but God that giveth the increase. Now he that planteth and he that watereth are one: but each shall receive his own reward according to his own labor."*

Here, Paul is talking about his one gift of evangelism. He was called to plant seeds. Apollos was called by God to nurture and water those seeds. The point is to use your gift or gifts; don't compare the importance of different gifts because it is God who makes them valuable:

We have different gifts, according to the grace given us. If a man's gift is prophesying, let him use it in proportion to his faith. If it is serving, let him serve; if it is teaching, let him teach; if it is encouraging, let him encourage; if it is contributing to the needs of others, let him give generously; if it is leadership, let him govern diligently; if it is showing mercy, let him do it cheerfully. (Romans 12:6–8 NIV)

We all have different gifts, but they are given to us by God. Whatever gifts, be it many or few, we are to use them as Jesus leads us. Listen to the Holy Spirit's guidance as to when and how to share them. Not for our glory, but for the glory of the One who saved us and leads us.

You may have many gifts or just one. The important thing to remember is gifts must be used. Like muscles, they need to be exercised. They are given to us by the grace of God and must be used for His glory. A gift performed in love is always of great value in the kingdom of God.

God will use our gifts for His higher purpose, and they will accomplish what He desires and achieve His goals. They will flourish and yield fruit, and we will be filled with joy because we were obedient in using them:

> *For my thoughts are not your thoughts, neither are your ways my ways, saith the Lord. For as the heavens are higher than the earth, so are my ways higher than your ways, and my thoughts than your thoughts. For as the rain cometh down, and the snow from heaven, and returneth not thither, but watereth the earth, and maketh it bring forth and bud, that it may give seed to the sower, and bread to the eater: So shall my word be that goeth forth out of my mouth: it shall not return unto me void, but it shall accomplish that which I please, and it shall prosper in the thing whereto I sent it. For ye shall go out with joy, and be led forth with peace: the mountains and the hills shall break forth before you into singing, and all the trees of the field shall clap their hands. Instead of the thorn shall come up the fir tree, and instead of the brier shall come up the myrtle tree: and it shall be to the Lord for a name, for an everlasting sign that shall not be cut off.* (Isaiah 55:8–13 KJV)

CHAPTER 8

THE FAITH OF A MAN

Jack Van Cleave was a wise and practical man. Things were done in order. An orderly process equaled an orderly outcome. Set goals, make a plan, follow the plan, adjust as you go, and see it to completion.

His faith was practical as well. He went to church every Sunday, served on the church council, walked with wisdom and integrity, and lived a good and righteous life.

Jack worked for the city of San Diego for thirty-five years, most of that in the Planning Department. When he retired after eight years as the planning director, he oversaw a staff of 167, with a budget of $7.2 million, in a city of a million people.[1]

During his employment with the city, he was also in the California Army National Guard. He attended artillery and armored officers' schools and rose to captain in the army reserve while also furthering his education in urban planning at San Diego State University, the University of San Diego, and the University of California Extension programs.[2]

---

[1] Jack Williams, "Jack Van Cleave; a treasured city planner," *The San Diego Union-Tribune*, April 12, 2003.

[2] Ibid.

He was my father. All this time, he also raised a family: his wife, Dorothy; a daughter, Debby; and three sons, Brian, Mike, and Kurt. He had a plan, and he worked that plan to completion.

I think that was why this practical man never completely understood his boys. Many times, he would ask me why I kept competing in sports when I would often be hurt. Oh, the countless times he asked us boys why we would do stupid things with no thought of the outcome.

I believe the apostle Thomas was a lot like my dad. A practical man. He's been labeled Doubting Thomas, but I think that is unfair. He was a realist; he was a man of faith, but a practical faith.

Danger ahead

By the time we first meet Thomas, it is late in Jesus's ministry. News had come that their friend, Lazarus, had died.

Jesus waited two days then announced to the Twelve that they would go back into Judea. By this time in His ministry, Jesus had been stirring up a lot of hatred among the Jews in Judea against Him; they had even tried to stone Him at one point, and now He wanted to go back there:

> Then after that saith he to his disciples, Let us go into Judaea again. His disciples say unto him, Master, the Jews of late sought to stone thee; and goest thou thither again? Jesus answered, Are there not twelve hours in the day? If any man walk in the day, he stumbleth not, because he seeth the light of this world. But if a man walk in the night, he stumbleth, because there is no light in him. These things said he: and after that he saith unto them, Our friend Lazarus sleepeth; but I go, that I may awake him out of sleep. Then said his disciples, Lord, if he sleep, he shall do well. Howbeit Jesus spake of his death: but they thought that he had spoken of taking of rest in sleep. (John 11:7–13 KJV)

Jesus was telling the disciples that there was still work to be done. Thomas would have understood this. Work while it is light so as to not stumble around in the darkness. This was practical; it made sense. They were going there to wake Lazarus up.

John 11:14–15 (KJV) tells us, *"Then said Jesus unto them plainly, Lazarus is dead. And I am glad for your sakes that I was not there, to the intent ye may believe; nevertheless let us go unto him."*

What Thomas didn't understand was that Jesus was saying that it was not time for Him to die, but to show that there is life after death. There was an appointed time for work to be done for the Father; this was the life of faith. Thomas now thinks that Jesus is saying Lazarus is dead, and it is time for us to die too. So he boldly stated to the others, "Let's go die too."

"Then said Thomas, which is called Didymus, unto his fellow disciples, Let us also go, that we may die with him" (John 11:16 KJV).

This wasn't pessimistic; this was practical faith. Thomas had decided to follow Jesus, and if that meant following Him to death then that made sense. He and Martha had missed the point. When Jesus finally arrived, Martha scolded Him about not being there sooner. If He had been there, Martha said, her brother wouldn't be dead. She knew Jesus could heal; she knew that Jesus would have healed Lazarus if He had come sooner. This was practical faith. She didn't know Jesus would bring Lazarus back from the dead; that was not practical.

But faith is not always practical; it's not always as we understand it. Sometimes it doesn't make sense; that's why it's called *faith*. Jesus said to Martha, *"I am the resurrection, and the life: he that believeth in me, though he were dead, yet shall he live: And whosoever liveth and believeth in me shall never die. Believest thou this?"* (John 11:25–26 KJV).

Which way?

At the Last Supper, as Jesus converses with His disciples in the upper room, we meet Thomas again. Jesus had just told them, *"I will be with you only a little longer... Where I am going, you cannot come."*[3]

---

3   John 13:33 (NIV).

Confused by this statement, Peter asked Jesus where He was going and why couldn't he come with Him. Not liking Jesus's response, Peter insisted that he would follow Jesus anywhere even if it meant his own death. Jesus then questioned his commitment and even predicted that Peter would deny Him three times before the rooster crowed that following morning.[4]

Jesus continued to teach them and tell them what was going to happen in the future:

> Do not let your hearts be troubled. Trust in God; trust also in me. In my Father's house are many rooms; if it were not so, I would have told you. I am going there to prepare a place for you. And if I go and prepare a place for you, I will come back and take you to be with me that you also may be where I am. You know the way to the place where I am going. (John 14:1–4 NIV)

By now Thomas is more confused than Peter, so he abruptly asked Jesus, *"Lord, we don't know where you are going, so how can we know the way?"* (John 14:5 NIV).

A fair statement: "Okay, Jesus, I get that we can't go with you, but you just said we know the place where you're going. No, we don't!"

A factual question: "Where are you going, and could you please draw us a map?"

The practical Thomas is probably thinking that if he can't come now then he needs to know how to get there later on when he does come.

Jesus then answered Thomas's question, *"I am the way and the truth and the life. No one comes to the Father except through me. If you really knew me, you would know my Father as well. From now on, you do know him and have seen him"* (John 14:6–7 NIV).

---

4   John 13:36–38 (NIV).

Where am I going? To the Father. What is the way? I am. How can you find it? Through me.

Thomas still didn't understand what Jesus was telling them; soon they would have to walk in faith. No longer would He physically be with them, showing them what to do and where to go. But He would be with them spiritually. Speaking to them through the Holy Spirit. The truth was in Him, and the way to God was through Him. The life that they were to live from now on would not always seem to be practical. It would mean hearing His voice in their spirit and obeying in faith.

No longer would Thomas set his goals, make his own plans, and follow them to completion.

Easter Sunday absentee

Three days after the death of Jesus, the disciples were locked in a room together in knee-knocking fear. It was the first Easter Sunday because Jesus had risen from the dead. He had appeared to Mary, and John and Peter had seen the empty tomb. Now Jesus makes His appearance to the apostles:

> *Then the same day at evening, being the first day of the week, when the doors were shut where the disciples were assembled for fear of the Jews, came Jesus and stood in the midst, and saith unto them, 'Peace be unto you.' And when he had so said, he shewed unto them his hands and his side. Then were the disciples glad, when they saw the Lord. Then said Jesus to them again, 'Peace be unto you: as my Father hath sent me, even so send I you.' And when he had said this, he breathed on them, and saith unto them, 'Receive ye the Holy Ghost: Whose soever sins ye remit, they are remitted unto them; and whose soever sins ye retain, they are retained.' (John 20:19–23 KJV)*

Jesus appeared to all His disciples except for two: Judas, who was dead, and Thomas, who was absent.

Why was Thomas not there? Why is he the only one missing?

Let's try to walk in Thomas's shoes.

Three years earlier, Thomas had left everything to follow a man whom he believed was the Messiah. Jesus was to be the next king of Israel. Thomas was one of His twelve disciples which meant surely, he would be a leader in the new administration. But now he had seen this man die and be buried. His goals, his plans, and his dreams have now died with Jesus. Thomas was upset, brokenhearted, and confused. He was disappointed and disillusioned; his friends had no answers, so why meet with them? His future had been crushed, so he was absent when Jesus appeared!

Think of all he missed! He missed the peace Jesus commanded over the disciples. He missed the joy of seeing Jesus alive again. He missed receiving the Holy Spirit. He missed the fellowship of his brothers in Christ.

We miss so much when we don't regularly fellowship with other believers. The Bible tells us:

> *They joined with the other believers in regular attendance at the apostles' teaching sessions and at the Communion services and prayer meetings.* (Acts 2:42 TLB)

> *They devoted themselves to the apostles' teaching and to the fellowship, to the breaking of bread and to prayer.*
> *Let us not neglect our church meetings, as some people do, but encourage and warn each other, especially now that the day of his coming back again is drawing near.* (Hebrews 10:25 TLB)

We miss the teaching that grows us to maturity in Jesus every time we fail to join others in worship. We miss the strength and courage that come from others who are facing the same struggles and temptations as us. We miss the presence of Jesus, His healing, and His empowerment through the Holy Spirit. We miss the hope of our victory over death.

No way!

Later that same day, we meet Thomas once more. When the others told him that they had seen Jesus risen from the dead, he replied, *"Unless I see the nail marks in his hands and put my finger where the nails were, and put my hand into his side, I will not believe it"* (John 20:25 NIV).

Thomas's faith is almost gone, but there is still an *unless*. He is skeptical, dejected, stubborn, and maybe a little arrogant, but there is still an *unless*.

God has a way of meeting us even in our unbelief. He makes a way even when we say, "No way" or "Unless." Jesus is about to do that for Thomas.

Believe

The following Sunday, Thomas joined the other disciples in their meeting place, and Jesus appeared again!

"A week later his disciples were in the house again, and Thomas was with them. Though the doors were locked, Jesus came and stood among them and said, 'Peace be with you!'" (John 20:26 NIV).

This time, Thomas is there. After Jesus greeted them, He went right over to Thomas. Jesus spoke directly to him. The risen Christ spoke the very words Thomas himself had spoken. *"Then he said to Thomas, 'Put your finger here; see my hands. Reach out your hand and put it into my side. Stop doubting and believe'"* (John 20:27 NIV).

Jesus then commanded Thomas to *"stop doubting and believe."* Thomas needed no more proof than seeing Jesus alive. He immediately jumped from doubter to believer. More than that, he saw Jesus as not just Savior but as the one true God and the Lord of his life!

"Thomas said to him, "My Lord and my God!" (John 20:28 NIV).

This practical man, with all his doubts and fears, finally understood what faith was. He found himself firmly planted on the solid rock of Christ. Then Jesus told him something that was directly pointed to us. *"Because you have seen me, you have believed; blessed are those who have not seen and yet have believed"* (John 20:29 NIV).

We are blessed if we believe without seeing. That is the true meaning of faith.

A realist

I think most men are realists. Like Thomas, they are practical. We will believe it when we see it with our own eyes. Maybe this is why Jesus showed Thomas the *proof* of scars in His hands and side. He was proving to this practical man that He really was the same Jesus Thomas knew before he witnessed Him die on a cross and be buried in a tomb.

Jesus met Thomas in the place of his unbelief. Like the father who came to Jesus for help with his demon-possessed son in Mark chapter 9:

> *And he asked his father, 'How long is it ago since this came unto him?' And he said, 'Of a child. And ofttimes it hath cast him into the fire, and into the waters, to destroy him: but if thou canst do anything, have compassion on us, and help us.' Jesus said unto him, 'If thou canst believe, all things are possible to him that believeth.' And straightway the father of the child cried out, and said with tears, 'Lord, I believe; help thou mine unbelief.'* (Mark 9:21–24 KJV)

Jesus will meet us where we have little faith, where we doubt in our heart, where we have unbelief, and lead us to *world-changing* faith if we are willing.

"Trust, but verify" is a rhyming Russian proverb. The phrase became internationally known in English after Suzanne Massie, an

American scholar, taught it to President Ronald Reagan, who used it on several occasions in the context of nuclear disarmament discussions with the Soviet Union.[5]

Like Ronald Reagan, I believe most men follow this advice.

Doubt is the robber of faith. When Peter jumped out of the boat, in faith, on that stormy night and began to walk on the water with Jesus, it was doubt that made him sink.

"Immediately Jesus reached out his hand and caught him. 'You of little faith,' he said, 'why did you doubt?'" (Matthew 14:3 NIV).

The scriptures contrast doubt and faith often:

> *Jesus answered and said unto them, 'Verily I say unto you, If ye have faith, and doubt not, ye shall not only do this which is done to the fig tree, but also if ye shall say unto this mountain, Be thou removed, and be thou cast into the sea; it shall be done. And all things, whatsoever ye shall ask in prayer, believing, ye shall receive.'* (Matthew 21:21–22 KJV)

> *But when he asks, he must believe and not doubt, because he who doubts is like a wave of the sea, blown and tossed by the wind. That man should not think he will receive anything from the Lord; he is a double-minded man, unstable in all he does.* (James 1:6–8 NIV)

But we are also told to *"be merciful to those who doubt"* (Jude 1:22 NIV). Why? Because we all have doubts. Doubts come often and sometimes relentlessly. Trials, suffering, temptations, and struggles test our faith and cause doubts to arise. Faith is a muscle that needs to be exercised. Faith is stronger when it is exercised without sight. *"Happy are those who have not seen and yet have found faith."*

If Jesus was just a man, He could show the way to the Father and die as a martyr. That Jesus could not die for your sins.

---

5 Wikipedia, "Trust, but verify," https://en.wikipedia.org/wiki/trust, but verify.

But Jesus was God, so He died as the sacrifice for our sins. His blood was shed so our sins would be covered, and we could have forgiveness. Believing in Him through faith and receiving Him as Savior and Lord bring us into the right relationship with the Father. Jesus has risen from the dead, proving to us that there is life after death, and faith in Him gives us eternal life:

> *Now faith is the substance of things hoped for, the evidence of things not seen.* (Hebrews 11:1 KJV)

> *While we look not at the things which are seen, but at the things which are not seen: for the things which are seen are temporal; but the things which are not seen are eternal.* (2 Corinthians 4:18 KJV)

They who believe shall see! The entire Christian faith is built on the lordship of the risen Christ. It is a choice of faith.

Jesus stands before every man, woman, and child with His scars visible and says, *"Put your finger in my nail scarred hands. Reach out and put your hand into my side. Stop doubting and believe. Happy are they who never saw me and yet have found faith."*

CHAPTER 9

THE CONFIDENCE OF A MAN
THE POWER OF COMPASSION
AND CONFRONTATION

Three hundred kids, counselors, and staff had gathered together from all over the northwest for a week of fun, craziness, and Jesus. It was time for junior high summer camp again. Each summer we would crowd into the small Foursquare Church camp. Camp Crestview was located in Corbett, Oregon, overlooking the beautiful Columbia Gorge, and I was its *inexperienced young* camp director.

One evening after the counselors and kids were bedded down for the night, the staff decided to go out for a late-night snack. We vacated the camp and drove down the hill to Troutdale, where Kruger's Truck Stop awaited our visit. Of course, all of us had to have the trucker's special: *three-bean chili,* heartburn in a bowl.

When I returned early morning, Dave, our head counselor, was waiting for me. He politely asked if he could speak to me, and I knew I was in trouble. Nobody likes confrontation, but Dave handled it like a pro. He was confident and compassionate, but he was direct.

"I have a problem with what happened tonight," he started. "I was unaware that the entire staff left the camp. Not only did I feel ditched, but no one let me know I was now in charge. What if there had been an emergency? You are the camp director. The director should go down with the ship or at least let the second-in-command know you're bailing out."

He didn't need to go on, and all I could respond with was, "You're right, I'm sorry."

I learned some valuable lessons that morning. I learned the importance of leadership; that it's no longer about you but those who have been put under your charge. I learned the value of confrontation; without it, I would have been left in the dark about my deficits as a leader. I learned about compassion—putting other people's feelings ahead of my own. I also experienced repentance and forgiveness again.

Woman caught in adultery

Jesus taught and lived these virtues, the ones that Dave patterned and taught me that night. We see these in the story of a woman caught in adultery in John 8:1–11 (KJV):

> But Jesus went unto the mount of Olives. And early in the morning he came again into the temple, and all the people came unto him; and he sat down, and taught them. And the scribes and the Pharisees bring a woman taken in adultery; and having set her in the midst, they say unto him, 'Teacher, this woman hath been taken in adultery, in the very act. Now in the law Moses commanded us to stone such: what then sayest thou of her?' And this they said, trying him, that they might have [whereof] to accuse him. But Jesus stooped down, and with his finger wrote on the ground. But when they continued asking him, he lifted up himself, and said unto them, 'He that is without sin among you, let him first cast a stone at her.' And again he stooped down, and with his finger wrote on the ground. And they, when they heard it, went out one by one, beginning from the eldest, [even] unto the last: and Jesus was

left alone, and the woman, where she was, in the midst. And Jesus lifted up himself, and said unto her, 'Woman, where are they? did no man condemn thee?' And she said, 'No man, Lord.' And Jesus said, 'Neither do I condemn thee: go thy way; from henceforth sin no more.'

The chapter opens with Jesus on the Mount of Olives praying. Early in the morning, He walked down the mount and into the temple courts where He began teaching the people. All of a sudden, His teaching was interrupted by a group of religious leaders, the teachers of the law and the Pharisees, dragging a woman to the feet of Jesus.

They told Jesus that they had caught this woman in the very act of violating the seventh commandment: *"You shall not commit adultery."*

As I have said before, I like to put myself in the middle of these stories to see what I would think and how I would feel if I were there, but this also brings up numerous questions like "How did they catch her in the very act? Was she set up and then used so that they could try to trap Jesus? Where is the dude who was also involved and just as guilty?"

It was definitely a well-thought-out trap. If Jesus were to forgive and acquit the woman then the Pharisees would accuse Him of despising and breaking the Law of Moses. If Jesus were to side with the Law of Moses and declare her worthy of death, then the Pharisees would report Him to the Romans as one who was assuming authority that belonged only to them.

What did Jesus do? He wrote in the sand. What did He write? I don't know.

Maybe He wrote the procedure they were to follow in accusing someone of this violation of the law? It was the husband's duty to charge her, and both guilty parties were to be punished equally. Maybe He wrote that they were just as guilty by ignoring the prescribed procedure?

Jesus then paused from His writing to say one thing to them, *"If any one of you is without sin, let him be the first to throw a stone at her."* And back to His writing. What did He write this time? I don't know.

Maybe He started writing the secret sins of the accusers? Maybe He wrote a Psalm. *"If thou, Lord, shouldest mark iniquities, O Lord, who shall stand? But there is forgiveness with thee, that thou mayest be feared"* (Psalms 130:3–4 KJV). All we know is that they all left; the oldest ones first.

Jesus had not overstepped the Law of Moses nor intruded on the authority of Rome. These accusers left, *shaking in their holy robes*, for fear of being exposed as the hypocrites they were.

Jesus didn't need to point out this woman's sin; everybody in the temple courts knew that. Instead, He offered forgiveness. In a compassionate confrontation, He told her He didn't condemn her, but that she was to leave her life of sin.

This woman, still at the feet of Jesus, must have been moved to tears of repentance, gratefulness, and love. It was the beginning of a new life for her, a life free from the bondage of sin and unrestricted service of her Savior.

Jesus hates sin and is not afraid to confront it, but He loves the sinner. This should be the spirit of all who follow Him. Christian love should be void of condemnation and quick to forgive.

The Pharisees

A number of times, Jesus confronted the Pharisees. On one such occasion, they asked Jesus about the disciples breaking the traditions of the elders concerning the washing of hands:

> *Then came to Jesus scribes and Pharisees, which were of Jerusalem, saying, 'Why do thy disciples transgress the tradition of the elders? for they wash not their hands when they eat bread.' But he answered and said unto them, 'Why do ye also transgress the commandment of God by your tradition? For God commanded, saying, Honour thy*

father and mother: and, He that curseth father or mother, let him die the death. But ye say, Whosoever shall say to his father or his mother, It is a gift, by whatsoever thou mightest be profited by me; And honour not his father or his mother, he shall be free. Thus have ye made the commandment of God of none effect by your tradition. Ye hypocrites, well did Esaias prophesy of you, saying, This people draweth nigh unto me with their mouth, and honoureth me with their lips; but their heart is far from me. But in vain they do worship me, teaching for doctrines the commandments of men.' (Matthew 15:1–9 KJV)

By this time in Jesus's ministry, He was a *rock star*. Thousands of people were following Him, listening to His teaching, and witnessing His miracles. Many believed that He was the promised Messiah. This enraged the Pharisees and teachers of the law. They were losing control of the people and their power. Their jealousy of Jesus motivated them to try and trap Him on numerous occasions.

Ceremonial purification was one of the most strenuously enforced observances and the rules in regard to this were numerous. The Pharisees taught that the neglect of one of these rules was punishable both in this world and the next. There were specific instructions concerning the washing of hands in the Law of Moses but washing before eating was not one of them. This was a strictly human tradition that had evolved in the Hebrew culture over the years. Jesus and His disciples were breaking the rules and spies made sure the Pharisees found out about it. So they felt they had a charge against the disciples and Jesus for not conforming to this rabbinic law.

Without hesitation, Jesus reminded them of the fifth commandment, *"Honor your father and your mother, so that you may live long in the land the Lord your God is giving you"* (Exodus 20:12 NIV). Then pointed out that they were guilty of breaking this commandment through the exercising of the rabbinic tradition of *corban*.

In this Jewish tradition, the word *corban*, which means "this belongs to God," could be used to designate their financial resources as not available for personal interests, like helping one's parents.

This was the height of hypocrisy. They were focusing on their rabbinic law of washing before eating and neglecting God's law of honoring their fathers and mothers.

Jesus then turned to the crowd and taught them what it meant to purify oneself.

"Jesus called the crowd to him and said, 'Listen and understand. What goes into a man's mouth does not make him 'unclean,' but what comes out of his mouth, that is what makes him 'unclean'" (Matthew 15:10–11 NIV).

Jesus's point in this confrontation was to free the people from the heavy burdens the Pharisees had placed on them. Out of love for the people, He forcefully confronted these men and with great wisdom pointed out the truth of God's word.

"Then the disciples came to him and asked, "Do you know that the Pharisees were offended when they heard this?" He replied, "Every plant that my heavenly Father has not planted will be pulled up by the roots. Leave them; they are blind guides. If a blind man leads a blind man, both will fall into a pit" (Matthew 15:12–14 NIV).

I see this as Jesus instructing us not to get into religious arguments. In the book of Titus, we are encouraged to avoid controversies and arguments because they are unprofitable. *"Don't get involved in arguing over unanswerable questions and controversial theological ideas; keep out of arguments and quarrels about obedience to Jewish laws, for this kind of thing isn't worthwhile; it only does harm"* (Titus 3:9 TLB).

Things will be sorted out by God the Father in eternity. We are not the judge, God is.

Matthew 7:1–6 (KJV) says:

> *Judge not, that ye be not judged. For with what judgment ye judge, ye shall be judged: and with what measure ye mete, it shall be measured to you again. And why beholdest thou the mote that is in thy brother's eye, but considerest not the beam*

that is in thine own eye? Or how wilt thou say to thy brother, Let me pull out the mote out of thine eye; and, behold, a beam is in thine own eye? Thou hypocrite, first cast out the beam out of thine own eye; and then shalt thou see clearly to cast out the mote out of thy brother's eye. Give not that which is holy unto the dogs, neither cast ye your pearls before swine, lest they trample them under their feet, and turn again and rend you.

You might ask, if we are not to judge and not to enter into quarrels, then when is it appropriate to confront someone?

Instructions on confrontation

The first thing that is important when deciding whether to confront another person is to make sure we are Holy Spirit driven and that it has been bathed in prayer.

The second thing to remember is to make sure we are properly judging the situation. Anyone who has been involved with confronting another person has probably heard this phrase, "Don't judge me." It's important to understand the different uses of the word *judgment*.

This word can be used as a *noun*, a *transitive verb*, or an *intransitive verb*. When used as a noun or an *intransitive* use of the verb, judgment is to act on an opinion. It issues a conclusion, a verdict, or a punishment. *Intransitive* judgment is to act as the judge.

Transitive use of the verb judgment is forming an opinion on something; this is discernment. Discernment is recognizing the need for change in a person's life.

Jesus went on to say in Matthew 7:15–20 (KJV):

Beware of false prophets, which come to you in sheep's clothing, but inwardly they are ravening wolves. Ye shall know them by their fruits. Do men gather grapes of thorns, or figs of thistles? Even so every good tree bringeth forth good fruit; but a cor-

rupt tree bringeth forth evil fruit. A good tree can-
not bring forth evil fruit, neither can a corrupt tree
bring forth good fruit. Every tree that bringeth not
forth good fruit is hewn down, and cast into the fire.
Wherefore by their fruits ye shall know them.

While not using the word judgment, Jesus taught the disciples both uses. *"Ye shall know them by their fruits."* You will know them (judge them) by their fruit. This is discernment. It is judgment using the *transitive* verb.

He then went on to say, *"Every tree that bringeth not forth good fruit is hewn down, and cast into the fire."* This is judgment using the verb as *intransitive*. They will be judged at the end of time by the judge, God the Father, and be thrown in the fire of hell.

When Dave confronted me that fateful morning, he was offering me his transitive judgment. In his opinion, I had fallen short of good leadership and friendship. He confronted me in love, and his judgment was right. Now, if he had said, "You are a terrible camp director, you should never direct a camp again, and I think you are going to hell," that would have been intransitive judgment, and the outcome would have been much different.

So intransitive judgment is the kind of judgment Jesus was speaking of when He said, *"Do not judge, or you too will be judged."*

Evangelism

The third important thing is whether the other person is a believer or not because the goals are different. With the unbeliever, the is goal is salvation through Jesus. The method is evangelism and yes, this is a form of confrontation. We are confronting them with their need to accept Jesus as Savior and Lord, repent of their sins, and receive forgiveness.

Jesus said:

> *Go into all the world and preach the good*
> *news to all creation. Whoever believes and is bap-*

tized will be saved, but whoever does not believe will be condemned. (Mark 16:15–16 NIV)

This is what is written: The Christ will suffer and rise from the dead on the third day, and repentance and forgiveness of sins will be preached in his name to all nations, beginning at Jerusalem. You are witnesses of these things. I am going to send you what my Father has promised; but stay in the city until you have been clothed with power from on high. (Luke 24:46–49 NIV)

Restoration

Confrontation of a believer must have the goal of restoration and forgiveness.

The scripture tells us, *"Brothers, if someone is caught in a sin, you who are spiritual should restore him gently. But watch yourself, or you also may be tempted"* (Galatians 6:1 NIV). This verse instructs us to go and gently confront a brother or sister caught in sin to restore them to fellowship. It must be done with much love and grace because we are not perfect.

In the Gospel of Matthew, we are told what to do if we offend someone else or if another believer has hurt us:

Ye have heard that it was said of them of old time, Thou shalt not kill; and whosoever shall kill shall be in danger of the judgment: But I say unto you, That whosoever is angry with his brother without a cause shall be in danger of the judgment: and whosoever shall say to his brother, Raca, shall be in danger of the council: but whosoever shall say, Thou fool, shall be in danger of hell fire. Therefore if thou bring thy gift to the altar, and there rememberest that thy brother hath ought against thee; Leave there thy gift before the altar, and go thy way; first be reconciled to thy brother, and then come and offer thy gift. (Matthew 5:21–24 KJV)

The enemy of our souls knows what unforgiveness will do to a Christian man; that's why he will give us every excuse in the book why we should not do it right. This verse tells us that we must stop our worship, leave our prayer closet, leave church early, and go and make it right with our brother whom we've hurt. In this verse, we are the offenders, the one who caused the hurt and the one who needs to be forgiven. In the next verse, we are the one who has been hurt.

"If your brother sins against you, go and show him his fault, just between the two of you. If he listens to you, you have won your brother over" (Matthew 18:15 NIV). We are to go and confront the one who hurt us with the goal of healing, forgiveness, and restoration.

In both cases, we are the one who is supposed to go and make it right. When we deal with conflict biblically, relationships are restored through God's grace, forgiveness flows, and healings happen.

Dave and I didn't know each other very well before that significant morning in August, but since then, we have become lifelong friends. As youth pastors, we ran many more camps together. We were business partners in a cabinet shop and rock-climbing buddies. All of this because he had the guts to stand up to me and point out my shortcomings as a leader.

He could have just gone to bed that evening and avoided the confrontation which, at the time, I would have done. Instead, he changed my life by showing me the power of a confident man. One who is not afraid to address a situation where he has been wronged. A man who will confront a person blinded by their selfishness with compassion, grace, and forgiveness.

CHAPTER 10

THE HEART OF A MAN
A FATHER'S LOVE

When my son, Brian Jr., was about four years old, he began getting sick. He had a little bump on the side of his chin that we didn't think was too serious. But in a short period, Brian got weaker and weaker, and the bump got larger. Finally, Brian collapsed in my arms, so I called my wife, Robann, and told her I was rushing Brian to the hospital.

My friend Larry met me at the hospital, arriving before Robann. They immediately took Brian into a room that they wouldn't let us come into. From the hall, I could hear my little boy scream as they attempted to put in an IV. Three times they jabbed his little arm unable to accomplish this routine procedure.

There were three important things I learned that day from this episode about the heart of a man and a father's love.

Deep within the heart of every man, God has created a capacity to profoundly love. This is a father's love, and it comes from the very heart of our heavenly Father. Even if a man has no children, it is still there waiting to reveal itself.

God's substitutional love

As Larry and I stood in the hall listening to my son cry out in pain, I remember thinking, *If only I could trade places with my son right now, I would do it in a heartbeat.* So I earnestly prayed, "God, is there any way possible that I could take Brian's place and receive his pain as my own?"

God wouldn't answer that request, but He showed me an incredible picture of His substitutional love for me.

You see, the Bible says:

> *When we were utterly helpless, with no way of escape, Christ came at just the right time and died for us sinners who had no use for him. Even if we were good, we really wouldn't expect anyone to die for us, though, of course, that might be barely possible. But God showed his great love for us by sending Christ to die for us while we were still sinners.* (Romans 5:6–8 TLB)

It also says, *"Yes, all have sinned; all fall short of God's glorious ideal"* (Romans 3:23 TLB).

We should all be in that hospital bed; the fact is all of us are sick with the disease of sin. But God loved us so much that He substituted His own Son in our place on that bed. Jesus voluntarily took upon Himself our sickness because He couldn't bear to see us in that condition. Just as I would have gladly traded places with my son, Jesus gladly traded places with us. He bore our sins, our sickness, our pain, on the cross.

Not only that, but He also went ahead and paid the hospital bill. In His death, He paid the penalty for us. The Bible says, *"For the wages of sin is death, but the free gift of God is eternal life through Jesus Christ our Lord"* (Romans 6:23 TLB).

As I stood with Larry in that hospital hallway, I began to understand deeper in my soul why God loved me and how much He really cared for me. He was showing me that my father's heart was a picture of the heavenly Father's heart of love for me.

The easy way out

Still, I couldn't bear to hear my son scream out in pain. That was enough; I ran into the room and grabbed my son. I shouted, "Get someone in here that knows how to put in an IV!"

A senior nurse came running in, settled me down, let me stay, and successfully put in the IV on her first attempt.

As I ran into that room, I was seriously tempted to just grab Brian and leave that place to go home. When he looked at me with eyes that said, "Daddy, why are you letting these bad people be mean to me?" I felt like this was the best option for my son. As I calmed down, I realized that staying was the best thing for my son. I couldn't help him get well, and I wouldn't be helping him by taking him home. That's when God gave me the second picture of His love.

When Jesus was arrested in the garden, Peter tried to defend Him by pulling his sword and cutting off the ear of the High Priest's servant. Jesus told him to put away the sword and then said something interesting in Matthew. *"Don't you realize that I could ask my Father for thousands of angels to protect us, and he would send them instantly?"* (Matthew 26:53 NIV).

Just a few hours later, after Jesus had been tortured, beaten, spit upon, laughed at, and nailed to a cross, in the next chapter of Matthew, we find another very interesting and seemingly contradictory statement. *"About three o'clock, Jesus shouted, "Eli, Eli, lama sabachthani?" which means, "My God, my God, why have you forsaken me?"* (Matthew 27:46 NIV).

Jesus on the cross crying out to His father was like Brian as I held him inside that hospital room, looking at me puzzled and in pain as if to say, "Daddy, why are you letting people hurt me?" In the mind of a bystander and even maybe in the mind of a son, the question can be raised, "What kind of a father would allow this?"

But God the Father knew the bigger picture. He knew that for the deliverance of all mankind, His Son must stay upon that tree. He also knew that soon all would be better for Jesus. Because shortly, Jesus would conquer the devil and take the keys to death, hell, and the grave. And after that, He would take His place for all eternity next to His Father in heaven.

Somebody help...please!

The doctor was on vacation, and no one at the hospital seemed to know what was wrong with Brian. Soon the lump on his chin was the size of a grapefruit, and talks about cancer were coming from the nurses. Brian was getting weaker by the day, and our fears were growing stronger hourly.

After a terrible week, the doctor came home, looked at the test results, and walked into Brian's room with a nurse and a tray. He cut into the infected lymph node, drained it, stitched up the cut, and told us we could take him home.

At first, I was mad; was that all it was? Why didn't someone do that sooner? Do you realize the kind of week we've had? But when I took Brian in my arms, all of my anger and frustration faded. I was taking my little boy home, and he was well! That was all that mattered.

On the way home from the hospital, I received the last revelation of the Father's heart of love, which was threefold:

1.   The solution is simple.
2.   Sin must be cut out.
3.   God wants a family reunion.

1)   *The solution seemed so simple.*

The solution seemed so simple; why didn't someone think of it the first day?

Most Americans, whether churched or unchurched, know one simple verse: *"For God loved the world so much that he gave his only Son so that anyone who believes in him shall not perish but have eternal life"* (John 3:16 NIV).

Another verse, which fewer know, is also found in the Gospel of John: *"But to all who received him, he gave the right to become children of God. All they needed to do was to trust him to save them"* (John 1:12 TLB). That seems so simple; why doesn't everyone do it? Maybe they're angry with God, frustrated with people, been hurt by religion, too busy enjoying their vacation? Maybe they think they are already a child of God without receiving Him?

Or maybe the cost is too high? John 1:12 goes beyond just believing; it says we must *receive* Him to become a child of God. The Greek word for *receive* here means *"to cling to, trust in, and rely upon."* Maybe it's just too expensive to actively and continually cling to Jesus, to trust our lives to Him, and to rely upon Him for direction daily?

I don't know. But I do know that for Brian and us, all of the other things faded into the background when we were reunited.

2) *Infection cut out*

Jesus did all of this for us so that we can be reunited with the Father. You see, sin has separated us from God, and there is only one way for us to get back home—it's through Jesus.

Like the doctor who cut out the infection allowing Brian to come home, Jesus wants to cut the sin out of our life. He already took our place on the hospital bed of sickness by His wounds, He already paid the bill on the cross by shedding His blood, and now He wants to cut out the sin by forgiveness.

John tells us, *"But if we confess our sins to him, he can be depended on to forgive us and to cleanse us from every wrong. (And it is perfectly proper for God to do this for us because Christ died to wash away our sins)"* (1 John 1:9 TLB).

3) *A family reunion*

That evening, as I rocked Brian in our La-Z-Boy chair and held him so tight, grateful thoughts of Jesus flooded my heart. We could have lost our son, but he was home well and safe in my arms. Our family was reunited once more. We were complete and whole once more.

A simple solution had to be found, and there was one doctor who knew the answer.

The Father knows the answer, and His heart wants a reunion with all who have been separated from the family because of sin. *"The Lord is not slow in keeping his promise, as some understand slowness. He is patient with you, not wanting anyone to perish, but everyone to come to repentance"* (2 Peter 3:9 NIV). If that's you, Jesus has traded places with you and taken the punishment for your sins. He's given you a simple solution and offered to cut the infection out.

Now it's up to you. You can take the easy way out and leave the hospital behind, or you can say, "Yes, Jesus, you know what to do. I give you the right in my life! Create in me a clean, new father's heart and renew a right spirit in me."

A MAN'S PLACE IN THIS WORLD

CONCLUSION

Satan has waged an all-out war against men in particular. The devil has inspired societies' massive attack on man's position, role, leadership, and even gender.

God established man, under Christ, as the head. He is to be the leader, protector, and cover over our society. Many people do not like this or agree with it, especially the devil, but that was God's plan from the beginning of time.

Satan knows how important man's role is in the church, family, and society. That's why he's worked so hard undermining that position.

Jesus is looking for men who will follow him unashamedly. (See Mark 8:38 and Romans 1:16.) Men who will love God with all their heart and love others as themselves. Men who will fight against the wiles of the devil. Men who will confidently stand in faith and cover their family, the church, and our society through prayer. Men who will walk in joy, using their gifts to further the gospel of the kingdom.

Are you that man?

Will you be that man?

ABOUT THE AUTHOR

B rian Van Cleave has been a minister of the gospel for over forty years. He retired from his position of senior pastor of the McMinnville Foursquare Church after twenty-five years of service. At the same time, Brian worked for Duniway Middle School as a special education reading teacher while coaching multiple middle school sports teams. He retired in 2018 but still teaches as a licensed substitute and continues to coach the seventh-grade tackle football team.

Brian is an accomplished guitarist and a *not-so-accomplished* golfer.

Brian and Robann have been married for forty-three years and reside in McMinnville, Oregon. They have three adult children and eight grandchildren.

CPSIA information can be obtained
at www.ICGtesting.com
Printed in the USA
JSHW052130300622
27448JS00007BA/290